Hammered

By

Dru Hammer

ISBN: 979-8-9909512-0-4 (Hard Cover)

ISBN: 979-8-9909512-2-8 (Paperback)

ISBN: 979-8-9909512-1-1 (Digital)

First printing edition 2024.
Cover photography by Paul Mobley.

Table of Contents

To my parents, Douglas and Donna Mobley,
who lived, walked, and talked their faith.
I miss them every day.

To my sons, Armie and Viktor Hammer,
without them… forget about it.
I couldn't be prouder or love them more deeply.

To all my future generations,
I hope to be their example to always love God first.

"I will give you a new heart and put a new spirit in you;
I will remove from you your heart of stone
and give you a heart of flesh."

— Ezekiel 36:26, NKJV

The Invitation

The beautiful moments I've shared with people have outweighed the responses from people who think I'm totally nuts. Someone had to win Billy Graham to the Lord, so I say, "Why not me, God?" I have been rejected and mocked more times than I can count—and probably many more I don't even know about. However, I will never stop, no matter what anyone thinks of me. I always answer to an audience of One. I don't apologize for who I am or for my Christian beliefs.

"God brings me a new cup of mercy every morning," as evangelist Aimee Semple McPherson would say. Wherever I am, I wake up praying, "God, I want to go where You want me to go. I want to be who You want me to be and do what You want me to do." There are some intermittent times of feeling defeated even amongst the victories.

All we take with us at the end of this life is what we did for Him.

We all fail and fall short. However, my story and my family's story are the epitome of not being able to fall any lower because we crashed and burned like marshmallows on an open fire. And yet, we rise. As a child, I learned that there is a heavenly, loving Father who not only holds us up in the tough times but He carries us when we need more.

I choose Jesus as my God, Messiah. I choose to take Him at His word. Some think He is a good prophet. Some think He is a fraud or never existed. I choose to believe He was a revolutionist who is the Messiah. He is either who He says He is or a madman. The best answer I can give is that He carried me through the biggest trial of my life- a shocking divorce from what I believed to be a wonderful 25-year marriage to my soulmate.

I probably went through my heartbreak differently than a lot of women. I've never been overly emotional. I had my moments where I was a slobbering mess, but I typically barrel my way through with a conviction of "oh, you can't take me down" attitude. Only my closest friends and family saw glimpses of the devastation I was going through, so don't expect a Hallmark book. To know me is to know that all my strength comes from the Lord.

I'm also a mother. I raised my two sons in the way I believe in. I brought my two sons, Armie and Viktor, into this world, and I love them so deeply. Their pain becomes my pain, and like all mothers, all I really want is for them to love God on their own and live a life of joy.

In everyone's life, storms come and go. In addition to divorce, my family survived the lies of cancel culture. Poor decisions were made. Personal agendas were placed before facts. For me, it all pushed me to my limit. Many times, I felt like I was drowning and was losing myself. However, I would never say that what I felt was my rock bottom was the same as someone else's. All of life's trials aren't equivalent. I can only be honest with you about how I felt during certain moments. My faith carried me through and then out of the devastation. Through everything, my family emerged more unified. I want to share how God's steady hand moved us to victory.

Life is hard enough with God, so I certainly don't want to try and make it on my own without God. There is a loving God who is there to help. Life will still be challenging, but we can have peace amongst trials and the promise of His protection. If God created us and this beautiful universe we live in, then I think He has a much better grip on my life than I could ever have alone.

When I was awakened to write this book, the clock read 5:55 a.m. The number five in the Bible stands for grace and unmerited favor. Grace and unmerited favor inspired me to write this book. All the miracles that happened in my life have made my faith much stronger, to the point that I'm probably unbearable at times. I'm so exuberant!

This book explains how accepting Jesus into my heart has worked in my life all day, every day. The beauty of this world is that we humans have the freedom to choose how we believe. Welcome to the world of my tremendous failures and His victories.

Chapter 1

Hammered!

Anytime your doctor wants a face-to-face, you know something is wrong. Something more than all the typical problems for a woman my age. I had gone in for a complete work-up because I had simply stopped sleeping. I was exhausted all the time. My body was always cold, and my husband started really getting on my nerves. We were best friends, and I could count the times we fought on one hand. Lately, however, he seemed short-tempered, and I was irritated, which was not typical in our 25 years together. Naturally, at my age, I figured I was going through menopause. Men...o...pause—that seems like the perfect word. After answering pages of questionnaires at the doctor's office, a personal consult, and blood tests, Dr. Wu called a week later with the results. He needed to meet with me in person.

Dr. Wu sat me down. All my numbers were off. My body temperature was running at 91 degrees. My thyroid had completely shut down. I was anemic and more. "What in the world is going on in your life?" Dr. Wu asked. "All these symptoms together could be due to severe stress." He suggested I go home and "meditate" to find out what was causing these symptoms.

I told Dr. Wu my form of meditation is praying to Jesus and that I would go home and do just that. With my head spinning, I drove home. I began going over a list of potential stresses. Money problems? Marital problems? Family health issues? No, no, and no. Even our children were in amazing stages in their lives. My oldest son Armie had booked his first big breakout role in the film "Social Network" and was madly in love. My son Viktor was excelling in the business program at Pepperdine University and had just fallen in love with Angie. As I kept going down my lists, I was stumped. My world seemed perfect to me.

Desperate, I prayed what may seem like a strange prayer to some. I asked the Lord to reveal to me if anything was going on in my spirit that my mind was not aware of yet and if that was why my body was having these reactions. Well, ask, and you shall receive.

I woke up the next morning and couldn't believe my dream. Actually, nightmare is the word. This may seem totally crazy, but it is the truth. I will spare you some of the gory details. In my nightmare, I saw a demonic sexual creature. I can still vividly see that demonic creature in my mind. He was the ugliest, most terrifying creature I have ever seen in my life. I saw and felt for the first time how cruel and evil the demon's intentions were. When I woke up, I was ashamed, thinking, "How in the world did my mind go there?" Then I had that aha moment. I realized the Lord allowed me to see how dark and evil the world is when you choose to follow that path instead of His straight and narrow one. That's when I knew that I was sleeping with a man who allowed demons into his life through adultery. And might I add, I have spoken and counseled with many women, and we all have the same story. The Bible says we don't fight against flesh and blood, but against powers and principalities (the dark, demonic world). The men who make these choices seem to be up to the same shenanigans. They try to make sure they leave the one they say they love with nothing and make them think it's all their fault.

What that dream revealed is that I was now sleeping with an enemy. I didn't want to believe it. No one wants to believe that the very person you have loved all your adult life could turn against you. It felt like a dagger went through my heart. I lay there in disbelief.

After that night, there was no doubt that the source of my physical distress was my marriage. There was darkness in my marriage. Because of my gory, vivid dream, I knew exactly what this darkness was. I also knew the ending would not be pretty. I woke up completely devastated. Surely, I'm mistaken. Were there signs? This wasn't the first time. Seven years into the marriage, I discovered my husband had been unfaithful. He promised me 19 years ago that infidelity would never happen again. My thoughts went on and on and on. I needed to confront my husband. Convinced as I was, I needed him to look me in the eyes and tell the truth. By the way, they never seem to come clean unless they are completely backed against the wall. He knew I heard from the Lord because I pursued a relationship with Him—and the Bible explains to us that He speaks to us in visions and dreams. That's how I knew.

I was churning all day long, trying not to believe what was revealed to me in my sleep. It was like I was walking around in a fog—just going through the day, numb from any form of emotion. I planned a nice dinner at home for the occasion. My husband and I used to go out to dinner every night, but who could have this conversation in a restaurant surrounded by strangers? I suggested we stay in, and I would cook. He came home, and I had a beautiful dinner all set out—candles, flowers, wine, you name it. After dinner and several generously poured glasses of "truth serum" for him, I came right out and asked how long he had been having an affair. The first time I found out he was unfaithful, we had small children. I didn't want my children to grow up without a father. I loved him, and he loved me. There was, as it seemed, sincere repentance then. Repentance means making a 180-degree turn, changing from your old ways in both the mind and heart, from self to God. Therefore, I fully forgave him. This time, it was different. It all turned out exactly like my dream, which was a nightmare. He, of course, denied everything at first. Then, as the dinner went on, he knew that I knew. Therefore, not only did it not turn out well, but it also turned ugly and fast. Once the darkness had been exposed, the devil reared his angry head, literally.

That night, I was terrified of the man I loved and devoted my life to. Everything changed so quickly. The man I never argued with, spoke with and texted 10 times a day, had dinner with every night, and had weekends together in Montecito—when in the heck did he even have time for affairs? I later found out he went to the Bel Air Hotel, the very place where we had date nights on Fridays with our friends. That simply shows just how crazy it all is. Where was this manual to tell me how to handle all this? That night, I slept on the opposite side of the bed. I would have fallen off if I had scooted over one more inch.

My mind was completely reeling. How did I go from having this loving husband who brought me pink roses every weekend, coffee in bed every morning, and was my best friend and family to not giving a flip or, even worse, telling me he was going to kill me? It was truly like being in a movie. I couldn't cry. I was too shocked. I had no warning and no time to prepare. Honestly, my mind couldn't even process the situation.

With my son Viktor home from college for Labor Day weekend, I couldn't even move into the guest room. I kept telling myself, "This will all end up okay." I didn't tell anyone right away, even Marty and Jenny, our house guests that weekend. I woke up the next morning, and like some would call a Stepford wife, I went down, made breakfast like nothing had happened. Inside, I was crushed. Staying in the same bed is impossible once you know you've been betrayed. It seemed unfeasible to even stay in the same house. All I could do was get out of town. I made a quick plan to head to Aspen. I look back with gratitude that I had that choice and a place to go.

The next morning, my assistant Jewels took me to the airport. I don't remember this, but she told me that when we drove out of the driveway, I stoically said, "This may be the last time I'm ever in this house with Michael living here." She said I was completely flat, with no emotion, almost robotic. We all have different ways of handling things. I've never been a huge crier. Sometimes, I'm actually concerned because I have such an ability to compartmentalize and push my feelings aside.

The office had made my travel arrangements for me, as usual. Numb, I walked up to the ticket counter to get checked in. It wasn't until I got to the gate that I looked down at my ticket. Coach. Wait? My seat was in coach? At the expense of sounding terribly spoiled, I was stunned. It's not that I minded flying coach—I just hadn't done it in our twenty-five years of marriage. Message received loud and clear. This wasn't about

4

my seat position, but my hanging-on-by-a-thread husband was establishing my position in his life now; I was no longer worth a first-class ticket or anything else to him. Crushed, I went to the bathroom to throw myself a pity party, as the numbness turned into "Is this really happening?" I walked into a stall and tried to cry quietly. Trust me, it was not a pretty Hollywood cry. Thankfully, I had the oversized Audrey Hepburn sunglasses on to disguise the red eyes with mascara running down my face. Getting myself together, I walked over to the gate and boarded the plane.

Once I took my seat, a young, beautiful Brazilian woman came and sat down next to me with a hunky man whom she had met in the airport bar. They were partying and raring to go. She turned to me and asked if I knew any great places to party in Aspen. Needless to say, I was not in the mood for that. I said, "I'm sorry. I'm not familiar with the bars in Aspen." I laid my head back and pretended to try to get some sleep.

Tap, tap, tap. "Well, do you know of some fun restaurants to go to with happy hours?" she asked. I suggested a few good restaurants but wasn't aware if they had happy hours. Tap, tap, tap. "Where do you hike in Aspen?" she asked. I answered and then asked if she wouldn't mind if I got some rest. Tap, tap, tap. NOW I just wanted to say, "Reallyyyyyy?!" Thankfully, I didn't. This time, she said, "For some strange reason, I feel like I can really talk with you." You've got to be kidding me! Apparently, my son Armie got all of his acting abilities from me because I was not in the mood for this, but clearly didn't show it.

She began to tell me her story. She said demons were attacking her at night. After the night I had, I understood the demonic attacks. She continued to open up, saying her mother was very upset with her for walking away from the Catholic religion. Naturally, she couldn't talk with her mother about this. She had been having terrors at night—the windows would fly open, a cold wind would come through, and her television would shake. I put that seat up, those two inches, and went to work. Now *this* I could be in the mood for.

I spoke to her from John 10:10 (NKJV), "The thief (devil) comes only to steal, kill, and destroy. I (Jesus) came that they may have and enjoy life and have it in abundance." I knew this was spiritual warfare, and the devil was terrorizing her in the night, robbing her of peace and joy. I have seen and know this stuff is real.

I explained that Jesus has authority over all darkness and is standing at the door of our hearts, knocking, waiting to be invited in. He will not come uninvited. As soon as we ask Jesus into our hearts, the darkness has to flee. Light overtakes darkness; darkness does not overtake light. I went into full "that will preach" mode and walked her through the entire plan of salvation. I wanted her to know that this was not about religion. Wars are fought in the name of religion. Jesus is about a relationship, and He loves us more than we can ever comprehend. She took my hand on the plane, and we prayed together. She asked Jesus to come into her life as her Lord and Savior.

Conveniently, the man she was with was knocked out next to us. There were no hindrances, and that's when I can get dangerous. I wanted her to have it all. We asked the Holy Spirit to fill her with the gift of praying in tongues. She already had the Holy Spirit when she asked Jesus into her life, but praying in tongues is one of the gifts we can have as well. Now, when the enemy tries to return (as he always does), she could take authority over the demons and pray out loud in tongues. Then they must flee, as stated in 1 John 3:8 and James 4:7.

Fortunately, I have never cared about winning any popularity contests. It was a good thing that day. We both began praying out loud in tongues as the Holy Spirit gave us utterance. Can you imagine how that must have looked or sounded on that plane? We didn't care. I have since received several emails from her saying how Jesus has changed her life and that she hasn't had any more attacks in the night.

God turned my sorrow that day into joy. I've always said if you are depressed or sad, go out and help others. You will find out there are people with situations so much worse than yours. When you minister to and help others, God heals your heart and theirs. It's a win-win.

Shame on me for that pity party I threw before the flight. I was sitting exactly where the Lord wanted me to sit. I put that seat two inches back and smiled. I also thanked the Lord. I said, "In the future, if you need me to share Christ with anyone in first class, I'm your girl." Now, on to Aspen.

Let's pray together

Jesus, You are the healer of the brokenhearted. This is a tough life with You; I can't imagine going through this life without You. You heal our hearts when we reach out and minister to others. Remind us in our dark days to continue to help others and to be mindful of the people You place in front of us. Amen

Chapter 2

Gal Pals

I said goodbye to my new friend on the plane. My distraction from her problems was over, and I was devastated over the end of my marriage but looking forward to seeing my spiritual godmother, Jean. She was not the warm and fuzzy person in my life. She was the definition of tough love.

Tough love was not what I particularly wanted during that time. But want and need are two different things. Tough love was what I needed. I had met Jean five years into my marriage. Armie was 3 years old, and Viktor was one year old. We were invited to a black-tie event by Libby, a friend from Tulsa. By the time we walked from the reception to the table, only two seats were left. I sat beside an exquisite, older woman dripping in jewels who reeked of class. We exchanged pleasantries. When the salad course was served, she turned to me and said, "Darling, I'm a Christian, and I always pray before meals. Would you like to join me?"

I almost fell to the floor. I knew people in Tulsa who prayed before meals. But in this Los Angeles, black-tie world, this was unheard of. I knew very few Christians in Los Angeles, and certainly not any who would be bold enough to pray out loud in the Beverly Wilshire ballroom. When Jean invited me to pray with her, she had me, like that memorable "Jerry Maguire" quote at hello.

From that day on, Jean has been my spiritual godmother. She taught me the ropes in a new, unfamiliar high-society world. At the time, I had no idea how the Lord would use her in my life—especially in the most critical of times. She would boss me around and tell painful truths, whether you wanted to hear them or not. She got her information from the Lord and was almost, always right. I say almost because after she learned why I flew up to Aspen to be with her, she basically told me to suck it up and go back home because my husband was a wonderful provider and good to me.

Let's just say that is a matter of perspective and generational. My generation didn't sweep things under the carpet and deal with them like Jean, who was over 30 years older than me. However, when my world was crumbling, and I didn't want to tell anyone in my family, I knew Jean would be there for me.

I went to bed that evening and completely fell apart, trying hard to believe that this was all just a bad dream. I hoped it would all disappear and we would return to our little, happy family. This new "revelation" was only 24 hours old. How do you process in 24 hours that the last 25 years of your life were built on lies?

That first night, over dinner, Jean told me she went to a wonderful little church called Crossroads. Even though I had been going to Aspen for years, I had never stayed over for a weekend. I usually popped in for a few days during the week to see her and then always returned home to be with my family for the weekend. When Jean took me to Crossroads, I kept praying for God to give me the strength to get through the church service like everything was okay. Isn't that what we all do? Walk into church with our pretty dresses on, smiling at everyone, asking, "How are you?" Then, when we're asked, we say, "Great." But sometimes, we're breaking on the inside.

When Jean took me to Crossroads, I had to walk into a church I had never been to, hoping to fake out everyone while wearing my Sunday best. Of course, when you show up with Jean, the "Grande Dame," you are escorted to the front row. Oh great.

Pastor Steve was in the middle of teaching a series on supernatural healings. He began to say that in the Bible, Jesus, before He was resurrected said, "Greater things will you do in My name. He commissioned us to go out and preach the gospel and lay hands on the sick, and they shall recover." (John 14:12, NLT)

Steve told the congregation that he had woken up that morning with a very strong unction from the Lord to tell a particular story on healing about his sister Shelley. Steve also said that in all his years of being in the ministry, he had never told this story before in the pulpit. He had my attention. Steve began.

When his sister, Shelley, was in middle school, she had a terrible case of scoliosis. Her spine was so curved that it was painful to even sit in class. Many days, she had to stay home and do her schoolwork from bed because sitting in those hard, wooden chairs was unbearable for her. The spine specialists said surgery was inevitable. Yet the surgery was so drastic that there was a chance of permanent nerve damage. There was a chance Shelley might never walk again.

Steve and Shelley's parents were raised in a religious home but never knew they could have a personal relationship with Jesus. His parents met some couples who had a Bible study and found Jesus on a personal level in that group of Christians. They started studying the Bible and fellowshipping with other "like-minded Christians." Their lives were being transformed. They'd never seen a supernatural healing, but through Bible study, they began to discover that Jesus did heal then and now. Not only that, but He also worked miracles through His disciples before and after He was resurrected, and He commissioned believers to go out and do the same. Steve continued.

One of the leaders in that Bible study had the gift of healing. The man didn't actually heal people, but God healed people through this man's faith. This man was a businessman, not a full-time 'minister. 'He still

10

conducted his business and supported his ministry from his businesses as he traveled all over the world, leading people to Christ and praying for the sick. Steve's parents decided to have this man pray over Shelley and ask Jesus to heal her before she had to go through this terrible and risky surgery. This man said to Shelley, "Don't look at me. I have nothing to do with your healing. It is Jesus who heals. I just have the faith to believe He will heal you."

Steve continued his story of how this man laid hands on Shelley's back and asked Jesus to touch and heal her. After he laid hands and prayed, Shelley said she felt a warmth go down her spine. This man felt that same heat in his hands. He believed Jesus had healed her and recommended she have another x-ray before going into surgery. The following week, Shelley returned to the surgeons and had another x-ray. Her spine was completely straight. To this day, over 45 years later, she has never had another problem with her back. Pastor Steve concluded his story by saying that this faithful man of God's name is Doug Mobley, who still prays for the sick. What. Did. He. Say. Excuse me. Wait. What?

I nearly fell to the floor. Doug Mobley is my dad!

Here I am, reeling from the recent discovery of betrayal in my marriage, and in a little church in the mountains, this pastor has an "unction" to share this story of all stories the only Sunday I was there. The Holy Spirit spoke to me as soon as Steve said who the man was. I heard, "Dru, I am going to heal your heart just as I healed Shelley's spine." I began weeping and said, "I hear you, God, loud and clear."

When the Holy Spirit spoke those healing words to me that day in church, I knew I would be okay. That is not to say I sailed through two years of divorce proceedings. I still had tough, brutal times. Even Jesus said, "In this life, you will have trials and tribulations, but I have overcome them all." John 16:33. Not some, but ALL.

I had that "something bigger than me" to help me through my divorce and other trials. He guided and comforted me when I didn't think I could scrape myself off the floor. If I only had myself to rely on, I'd be in a heap of trouble. I'm just smart enough to make Jesus the chairman of my board.

After a week in Aspen, I said goodbye to Jean and thanked her for her hospitality. Eventually, I shared the news with Jean that my marriage was ending. She said she already had figured it out. I valued her presence, how she cared for me, and for always being a spiritual mother.

I had to return to Los Angeles and face the inevitable. I was scheduled to finally have lunch with a woman I had met, Lesley, the day after I flew home. She was a new friend. I still wasn't in the mood to put on that happy face.

Lesley was the publicist for Armie's first movie he booked, *Billy: The Early Years*. This movie was my sign from the Lord that Armie was sitting on the chair the Lord had chosen for him. The movie was about Billy Graham's humble beginnings and how he was called and grew into a worldwide evangelist. I always told Armie that playing Billy Graham in his first role was a sign to me, which I needed as I had seen what a jungle it is in Hollywood.

For six years, I kept running into Lesley at Angelus Temple Church when she was visiting Los Angeles from Nashville. Every time, we would say, "Let's meet for lunch," but we never seemed to get around to doing it. Finally, we had a date on our calendars to meet for lunch. I was going through so much emotional chaos. I wasn't ready to share what was happening in my life with Lesley or anyone for that matter. To make matters worse, Lesley called to see if it would be okay if she brought a friend of hers to join us. Ugh. But then again, how could I cancel when we had tried for years to get together? I decided to just suck it up, go and put on a happy face, and then cry when I got back home.

Lesley brought her friend Lou, who is one of the top business managers in the entertainment and sports world. Lou is also a pastor's wife to an incredible man, Rob, from Calvary Chapel in Nashville. After an hour of talking with these two Godly women, I calmly said, "For some reason, I trust you two, and I have to get something off my chest. I just found out last week that my husband has been having affairs for years, and I am devastated." Well, these two powerful business women kicked into drive and took off on my behalf.

It turns out Lesley had been through something like myself, and Lou had counseled her through the entire process. I explained that my husband and I had been married for 25 years. We are best friends and soul mates, and I know it will all turn out okay. Lou looked me straight into my eyes and said, "I've been through this with so many of my friends, and it will not be amicable unless there is true repentance."

Lou went on to say that my husband was no longer my best friend. He betrayed me, and best friends don't betray each other. Unfortunately, Lou was right. Those two ladies tag-teamed me and cared for me like we had all been best friends our entire lives. Lesley had been there, and Lou carried both of us through with her no-nonsense, no-fluff approach. Lou even met with my husband and tried to convince him that you don't treat the wife of your youth with contempt. Michael's reactions only convinced Lou even more that this would turn out just as her other client's marriages had. Lesley and Lou were two rocks in my life, and I couldn't have made it without them. As busy as the two were, they would always take my late-night calls and listen to me crying and ranting about how unfair this was. I was so grateful God was sending new friends to me, but I was also trying to adjust to Michael's absence as much as possible, which was very difficult. Spiritually, I was walking with the Lord, but my physical body was reacting to the marriage ending. I went to my doctor for a check-up. He noticed I had lost a lot of weight and didn't look healthy. My skin was literally gray, my hair had turned white on top, and I was all skin and bones. I was so depressed. I had absolutely no expression or diction in my voice. I was as flat as a pancake.

My doctor asked what was going on in my life. When I explained how I was going through a devastating divorce, he recommended putting me on antidepressants during this period. I told him I didn't want to do that. For me, if the Lord had told me He was going to heal me, I had to rely on Him totally. I had to get through the pain and face it head-on through several years of devastation, heartbrokenness, loneliness, and many tears.

There is no easy way to handle heartbreak; the devastation is real. But as a believer in a God who loves us, I knew I could count on Him always showing up even when my circumstances around me were downright dismal. He's waiting for us to turn to Him. I just knew I had to stand on the promise the Lord gave me that He was my healer. But it required a lot of work on my part. I had to hone in on Him and seek His face morning, noon, and night. This meant I couldn't medicate or numb the pain as much as I wanted to.

I knew I had to pick myself up, but I also knew that it would take some time and, again, a lot of hard work. The divorce seemed inevitable even though I prayed continuously for a different outcome. Even with my faith intact, family, and a small group of friends, I still felt like I was ascending to rock bottom. God promises us many wonderful things, but He never promised we would have a perfect life. So, I held on. What was about to come, I could have never imagined.

Let's pray together

God, never in a million years would I ever think that I would be going through a devastating divorce. Thank you for sending loving people into my life to help me through these difficult times. We are not meant to go through heartbreak alone. You restore all. Amen

Chapter 3

A God of Miracles

From family traditions to business ventures to simple daily life, my parents, Donna and Douglas Mobley modeled a God-centered life. Interestingly, neither of my parents was raised in an overtly Christian home. When they were taught that they could have a personal relationship with God as young adults, they went for it. My dad always said, "The longest distance in the world is 12 inches—moving God from a head-knowledge down to a personal heart experience."

When I was growing up, I vividly remember how my father used to go to our guest quarters in the evenings and pray, seeking God. I would come home from school, and my mom would have her bible and concordance out, studying the Word. They both pursued a strong, personal relationship with Jesus. To me, *that* is a rich heritage.

My parents were both raised in very poor homes. My mother's father passed away when she was 12 years old. My mother rarely spoke about her childhood, but once, she told me some difficult things she remembered. My grandmother would send her down to the local pub to bring her father home, who was usually in a drunken stupor. She was his favorite; her mother knew he would do anything for his daughter. My mother took her three daughters to Chicago and wanted a driver to take us to the south side of town so she could show us where she grew up in the apartment projects. We couldn't find a driver who would take us. It is such a dangerous area. Her father died from alcoholism. When he passed away, the family of three children were left penniless.

Thankfully, my grandmother had a nursing degree. They moved from the Chicago projects to Austin. It was there where she would walk miles to work the night shift at the hospital. She worked all night. Then, she walked home early in the morning to get her children off to school—only to do it all over again the following evening.

My dad's father was a butcher and walked two miles each way to the butcher's shop during all kinds of weather. Every night at dinner, he would talk about how he hoped they would have enough to get through that month. The "I walked miles to and from work" stories were true in both my grandparents' lives.

That desperation did something to my dad. He became very ambitious and always said, "I will never raise my family in that way." He started as a young boy collecting Coke bottles and running paper routes—you name it, he did it. My parents were the first generation in their families to go to college. To put himself through college, my dad got a partial scholarship to play basketball and started a business doing laundry for his wealthy fraternity brothers. He was also the houseboy at a sorority in exchange for free food.

My mother received a full academic scholarship through Phillips Petroleum Corporation. If not for the scholarship, she would have never been able to attend college. God had a plan for my parents to meet.

They met in the Pi Beta Phi sorority house at Oklahoma State University, where my dad was the houseboy. They fell madly in love and got married at 20 years old.

My mom eventually had to quit school to work to put my dad through college. My mom was so smart that within six months of her secretarial job at the university, she was promoted to be the personal secretary of the university's president. When she would go to the local laundromat, all the women would tell her how foolish she was and that her husband was going to dump her as soon as she paid for his degree. Sixty-seven years later, they were more in love than the day they were married.

My dad had always been driven, maybe to a fault. He worked seven days a week to get ahead, much to the exclusion of his family. He had no peace until he felt like he had "made it." He didn't realize that peace doesn't come from how many zeros you have in the bank or how "successful" you become in the world's eyes. Eventually, he learned what inner peace meant.

He met some young Christian businessmen who shared how he could have a personal relationship with God. At first, my dad didn't fully understand. Then, the men took him to lunch one day to talk with him about God. When they joined hands and prayed to bless the food, my dad was so embarrassed that he wanted to crawl under the table. Though my dad was uncomfortable that day, he saw they had something he didn't. They were businessmen like him, but they had peace.

Years before meeting these men in Tulsa, my parents were invited to a dinner party at a fraternity brother's house, where they had all taken jobs in Dallas after graduating from college. My dad didn't know them very well as he had little time for social things during college. He was too busy working three jobs. After a lot of drinking and partying, the men all put their keys into a bowl, and the women, blindfolded, picked out a set of keys. Each woman was supposed to go home with the man who owned that set of keys. Imagine the shock! My parents had never heard of swingers, but as soon as my dad "keyed in" to what was going on, he grabbed my mom's hand, his own set of keys, and they left. "We will never live like that," my dad told my mom. "This is not for us, and we will find like-minded friends." After seeing these two dichotomies, he knew which life he wanted for his family. As uncomfortable as he was seeing men pray openly in public, he called the Godly men together and asked them how he could find Jesus in his life. He began going to a men's Bible study with them to learn the character of Christ. If you are going to follow someone, you have to know their character, which is the purpose of reading the Bible. These men and their wives, whom I will always be eternally grateful for, became my parents 'peeps and changed the entire paradigm of their lives. I often think of those men just serving God and sharing Christ at lunch. Little did they know how they literally changed generations in my family. From that point forward, my parents modeled a trust in God. Their futures didn't look much brighter than getting jobs and "making it," but God had a better plan. He knew their hearts. He knew they would use the money they were blessed with to go out and bless others.

God started giving my dad ideas on how to start businesses without an extra dime in the bank. My mom says she never doubted that my dad would succeed, even when they were barely getting by. There's a saying that it takes money to make money. When you start a business on your own, it's certainly easier with money or investors. They had neither. Yet God can do the impossible. Sixty years ago, my dad made $5,000 on the first house he contracted. The first thing he did was write a check back to the Lord for $500. It was a tithe check. A tithe is giving what the Lord has asked of all of us—giving Him back the first fruits, the first 10 percent of profits. Tithing is an act of obedience and thanksgiving to God for blessing us. He said he had never felt joy like that in his entire life and fell to his knees and wept like a baby. God had blessed him to be a blessing.

Soon, God began speaking to my father about a healing ministry. During that time, a man asked my dad to please come pray for him, as he was about to have a major surgery. If he had this surgery, he would never be able to fly commercial jets again. This was his dream since childhood. Neither of them had ever seen a miraculous healing at that time, but they kept reading Biblical accounts of Jesus healing people. They began to believe that He is "the Lord God who does not change." (Malachi 3:6) and that He still heals today. My dad drove to see this man in the hospital, who was about to go in for surgery the next morning. This was all so new to my dad. He tells of not even knowing how to pray. So, he laid his hands on him and said a simple prayer of asking Jesus to heal him. They both felt an electricity going through their bodies. Believing Jesus had performed a miracle, my dad suggested the man have another x-ray before having surgery. Sure enough, the man was healed and flew for another 35 years.

After my dad got back into his car that night, the Holy Spirit's presence surrounded him. God spoke to him and said He was calling my dad to pray for the sick, and Jesus would heal them. My faithful father was all in, but there was a stipulation. He asked the Lord to bless his businesses so he never had to ask for a dime. He wanted to pay for every expense incurred in the ministry. There's nothing wrong with taking up offerings to pay for ministry expenses, but my dad just had the faith to believe God could bless his businesses to cover everything.

As amazing as this was, it seemed very 'out there 'for many Christians— even in Tulsa, Oklahoma, the buckle of the Bible belt. When you aren't raised around the supernatural power of God, these stories do sound crazy. God made some huge changes in our family. By this time, my dad was a land developer and owned some banks and lumber yards. He felt like God was going to lighten his business load so he and my mom could have more time for ministry. After the encounter with the Holy Spirit that night in dad's car, the Lord brought several buyers to his office and sold a few of his banks and lumber yards. My parents tithed from the sales, set up their foundation, and started their ministry, all while continuing in business.

It just so happened that the Tulsa papers picked up the scoop when my dad sold his interest in one of the larger downtown banks, much to his chagrin. My dad was the most private, humble man. For example, every year when he bought a new car, he bought the same color and model, "so no one knows I bought a new car," he would say.

You can imagine that he certainly didn't want his business dealings in the paper. Definitely not on the front page of the *Tulsa World*. It said, "Tulsa businessman sells bank to begin a healing ministry." The morning the article came out, I happened to be spending the night with one of my best friends, Kay. Her parents woke us up and said, "Dru, your dad is on the front page of the paper this morning." That was social suicide for a senior in high school, even in the Bible belt. I was homecoming queen that year, but after that article came out, I was completely rejected by all my friends. I knew the truth and what was important in life at the time, but I kept thinking, "Couldn't God and my parents have waited until I had graduated from high school and gone off to college?" It's amazing how self-absorbed we can be in life.

Right after the article in the paper came out, my dad began receiving calls from people who had read about his ministry. That big fat phone book was causing our phone to ring off the hook. A woman with stage 4 cancer called him. She had gone through months of radical chemotherapy. The oncologists had done everything they could possibly do. My mom was helping my sister Mel with her homework. As my dad felt it was inappropriate to be in a woman's house by himself, he asked if I would come along with him to pray for this woman. Even though I wasn't exactly happy with the timing of his ministry launch—worrying about what others thought of me—I went. It was a freezing cold night, and it was snowing. The woman lived alone in an old, broken-down trailer on the other side of town. Cancer treatments have come a long way from 45 years ago. She was sent home to die. Jesus was her only hope. When we arrived, she was in one of those old-fashioned house coats like my grandmother used to wear. She was completely bald, and her skin was drawn and grayish in color. I remember the smell of sickness in that trailer. We shared with her how much Jesus loved her. My dad always made sure the people had the Lord in their hearts, not just in their minds. My dad laid his hands on her head and asked Jesus to touch her and heal her. As I looked up, I saw hair starting to grow back on her head. I couldn't believe my eyes. The Lord softly spoke to me and said, "I am a God of miracles. Do not ever doubt My power."

How in the world could I ever deny it after what I saw?

My parents gave me the gift of seeing Jesus do countless physical miracles, but they also gave me the gift of their Godly example, especially when it came to forgiveness. Jesus heals hearts through forgiveness. My dad was in an oil deal when he found out one of his partners was cheating him and manipulating the books. My dad was devastated because they were friends before they were business partners. Dad took his friend to lunch and asked his friend to forgive him for harboring unforgiveness.

When dad told me the story, I didn't understand why he was the one who had to ask for forgiveness. It didn't seem like he did anything wrong. Now, after my own heartbreaking trial in life, I get it. Unforgiveness needs forgiveness just as much as the offense. Jesus paid the price and forgave us. Therefore, we are to forgive others… period. That doesn't mean it is easy. When my dad prayed about his situation, the Lord told him to forgive his friend and let it go. He would then restore what was stolen. And that is exactly what happened after that fateful lunch. The hardest part of forgiveness is we want to take revenge and make sure the offender suffers for how they wronged us. Is that just me? Maybe not.

I remember that inside my father's wallet was a worn and torn hand-written note from his mother. It read, "May this wallet never be empty to the glory of God." Having money isn't to the glory of God. Being able to give is to the glory of God. My dad always carried a stack of hundred-dollar bills in that same wallet. Every day of my life, I would see him walk up to people, having heard from the Lord, and hand them money. He'd pray and share with them how Jesus loved them. I could see the angels rejoicing over the lost sheep being found.

When we were young, my sisters and I didn't always appreciate what our dad was doing. Almost every time we were out to dinner, the Lord would put in dad's heart a desire to help people in the restaurant. He would walk up to a table and share Christ. Before we left the restaurant, he gave them money and secretly picked up their dinner bill. As a teenager, it seemed to be a nuisance as we waited and waited. We just wanted to get home to our friends. Looking back, I appreciate the lessons of generosity my dad taught us girls.

My parents always said, "Put your money where your mouth is." I ran every day with my Dad at the running trails in Tulsa on the Riverside. We ran four to five miles every day except Sunday with our running group.

Joel, a local Jewish Businessman, was in our running group and one of my dad's best friends. My dad ministered to him daily. Joel kept showing up. As my dad ran, he would stop and talk to people about Jesus, even on the running trail.

One day, I was off at college, and he ran past a man with a horrible cleft palate; half of his upper lip was deformed, and his teeth were mangled.

My dad stopped and went back and shared Christ with this man who could hardly talk because of his mouth. He told my Dad he knew Jesus and taught a small bible study at his Hispanic church. He wanted to be a pastor. My dad knew he couldn't be a pastor with his speech difficulty. So, secretly, my dad found a surgeon specializing in cleft palates. He called the man's pastor and asked if there was someone who could get this Sunday school teacher to Dallas, and my dad would take care of all his expenses and pay for the several surgeries he would need to fix his mouth. We heard through the years this man has a thriving church leading many to Jesus and to this day knows God. The day the Lord took my dad home, my sisters and I could only imagine how many thousands of people in Heaven rejoiced because of my parents' choice to serve Him first.

I was amazed at how the Lord has blessed others through the obedience of my parents. Their foundation has supported countless people.

Monthly checks were sent anonymously through churches and ministries. Hundreds of widows and single women who struggled to raise children on their own would receive those checks each month. Through the foundation, my dad has put more braces on children's teeth, paid for the surgical repair of cleft palates, scholarships to Christian universities, supported countless ministries, given land to churches, and helped finance their building projects. My parents went all over the world leading people to Jesus, praying for the infirm to be healed while underwriting every penny.

I believe it's important to note that when my parents traveled the world with their healing ministry, they were extremely sensible. Those ministry trips were anything but luxurious. They would fly using points, share meals, and book nice but less expensive hotel rooms. My dad would always say, "This is God's money. We have to use it prudently and wisely."

My parents also modeled for us how to apply our faith in practical ways. After my mom had a kidney transplant, she was dependent on an anti-rejection medication called Prednisone for the rest of her life. We still prayed and believed God would heal her from her dependency on this drug, but the Lord heals supernaturally also through doctors and medications. The kidney my sister Lisa gave her proved strong for 20 years. The surgeons told mom she would be "lucky," although we don't believe in luck, to get 10 years from this kidney because she was in her mid-60s. When she met the Lord, her frail body gave out – but not from kidney failure. It was just her time. When my mom was 40 years old, she was diagnosed with polycystic kidneys. As there was no cure, her doctor told her she would not live to see her 50s. My mother passed away at 86, and her kidney function was in full swing.

One of the side effects of Prednisone is, among other things, memory loss. This was very difficult for my mom, who always had a very sharp mind. A few years after the transplant, as her memory seemed to get worse, we would call mom, and she would tell us the same stories she told us the last time we called. During that time, my son Armie and I surprised my parents in Budapest while they were on a ministry trip. While riding the train to a meeting, we noticed my mom had her Bible out and was talking to herself as if she was reciting something. When we asked her what she was doing, she responded, "My memory started fading, so I asked the Lord to heal and restore my memory. I believe when we ask God for something, we also need to do our part. We can't pray for a job and not go out on interviews. I began using my mind and memorizing the Bible."

At that point, she had memorized over 10 complete chapters in the Bible—many being a few pages long. Armie and I were astounded when she recited chapter after chapter, word for word, to us.

It's a good thing my parents came to know Jesus when I was a young child. I would have been a terror if they hadn't raised us in the ways of the Lord. Even so, of the three girls, I was the most difficult, most stubborn child. My older sister, Lisa, is extremely driven and smart. Lisa runs circles around me. Then there's my younger sister, Mel, who we call Honey Bee. She's also smart and the kindest person you will ever know. And finally, there is me. What can I say? I'm the one who was and is always pushing the limit. I was bossy and never a great student. I was good at working the system, though. My interest was just having fun—my way.

As a child, I would not go to sleep, eat, or play when anyone else wanted me to. I absolutely refused to sleep, much to the exasperation of my parents. When I was only two years old, I was not about to sleep in a crib. I would lay there for hours and kick and kick until one night, my crib fell apart. With no crib to keep me contained, I would roam around for hours at night. My parents couldn't keep me in bed. My mom called the pediatrician. It was suggested to her that she put anything dangerous away and just let me wander around until I wore myself out. Surely, I would eventually fall asleep. Yeah, not so much. In kindergarten, I got a bad report card. It was marked with "does not play well with others," among other issues. My friends wanted to abide by the rules, but I wanted them to come and do what I wanted them to do. My rules.

I was such a pill. I refused to eat if I didn't like the food my mom made for dinner. My parents would make me sit at the table until I ate it. Hours later, completely discouraged, they would let me get up to play. I eat anything and everything these days and wouldn't think of leaving good food on the table. There has got to be a happy medium. But I haven't found it yet.

I was the daughter who loved sports like my dad. I was the son he never had—truly a tomboy. My mom bought a huge cowbell and would ring it from the front porch to tell me it was time to come home for dinner because I was running around the neighborhood. I was playing ball and jumping on trampolines with the neighborhood boys. I hated girly things. My mom gave me a doll one year for Christmas. I was so mad about getting a doll I threw it against the wall and refused to touch it again. Once I was playing house with a neighborhood friend. Of course, I was the boss, the mom, and she was the baby. I knew exactly what I was doing, even as a young child. I tucked her in and knelt to say prayers with her before bedtime. Then, I got up, bent down, and directed her, "Now scream!" Certainly, an interesting way to 'play 'mom.

What in the world do you do with a child like that? My dad refused to have another child after me, but my mom knew she wasn't finished with her family and finally talked my dad into one more child. Once my sister, Mel "Honeybee", came along, none of us imagined what we would have ever done without her.

My dad was truly the spiritual leader of our family, and my mom was the quintessential mother. She baked fresh cookies for us every day when we got home from school. On Mondays, she baked fresh bread for the week. And for heaven's sake, she even gardened in a skirt. I don't remember ever coming home when my mom wasn't there for me, even in high school, to ask about my day. Since I was a tomboy, my dad was always my best friend and hero. We played tennis together and ran together almost every day. He has a great sense of humor, and I loved listening to him talk about his business developments and banks.

My parents didn't lay down a bunch of rules. Their Godly example took all the fun out of rebelling. When I was older, my dad would say, "Honey, I'm not going to give you a curfew or tell you where you can and can't go. I trust you. Just call us and check in to tell your mom and me you are okay." I never wanted to disappoint them.

My fondest memory was walking into the kitchen at night and finding my parents swing dancing together to fifties music from their portable radio. Until my dad died, I still loved dancing with him. It was truly a Norman Rockwell childhood with Christ in the center. I figured everybody had a happy home like ours. I was wrong. I ended up with a man who came from a drastically different and dysfunctional home life, but the Lord put me there. It was time to see how the other half lived.

Let's pray together

God, when our earthly fathers fail us, You will never fail us, and You will overcompensate and be their Father. I pray that people s hearts will be opened to receive Your love and believe that You are a miracle-working God. Amen

Chapter 4

Divine Encounters

Unlike my sorority sisters at Oklahoma State University, I wasn't out to get a ring by spring. I wanted to see the great, big world.

I had been dating nice guys, but nothing serious. One of them, John, had invited me to play in a mixed-doubles tennis tournament in Houston. After losing in the semi-finals, we took a flight back to Tulsa a day early. There were no direct flights, and we had to touch down in Dallas first. As we sat on the plane, my future husband Michael walked in. It's hard to describe, but as he walked on the plane, I had a strong feeling from the Lord that I was going to marry him. Funny, I wasn't even looking or wanted to get married.

Meanwhile, I was sitting next to another man. I have always talked to God like I'm having coffee with a friend, as He *is* my best friend. My parents taught me that prayer is simply talking and spending time with the Lord. He is a personal God who wants a relationship with his children. I remember the moment so clearly. "God, if this is the man you have for me, then You will have to do some fast work. This flight is only an hour long, and no seats are open near us." As if God really needed my help.

I later found out that Michael had been working in Tulsa at City Service, which was a domestic oil company that his grandfather's company had acquired. At the time, I didn't know Michael's grandfather was a legendary American businessman, Dr. Armand Hammer. I was so young and taken by Michael that his high-end and famous pedigree would not have registered with me anyway.

Michael was headed back to Tulsa after spending the weekend with his sister in Dallas. He had missed his earlier flight, and only one seat was left on our flight. He barely made it. When he got on the plane, the only seat left was a middle seat two rows behind John and me. Now Mr. future husband, a very tall man, couldn't fit into the middle seat. He politely asked if anyone would mind trading him for an aisle seat. Who trades an aisle seat for a middle seat? Thankfully, he got a taker—and my attention. Lo and behold, the woman next to me said she would be happy to trade.

The three of us talked the entire way home to Tulsa. When we landed, it was pouring down rain. John went to get the car while I waited for the luggage. Michael walked over and asked, "Is that your boyfriend or fiancé?" Forgive me, Lord! I answered, "Oh, heavens no!"

Given all clear, Michael invited me to lunch the next day. Lunch turned into dinner, into lunch the next day, into dinner. You get the picture. I think he was so taken by me because I was different from the wild surfing girls he grew up with in Southern California. I thought he had lost his mind when he asked me to stay over just a few nights knowing him. The stock I'm from, we didn't do that.

As if that weren't enough, I started sharing Christ with him. When he heard how important Jesus was in my life, he was flooded with childhood memories of his grandmother from Russia, Olga Von Root. Olga, a very famous Russian stage actress and singer, was a gorgeous woman. He must have gotten his looks from her. She also loved Jesus and used to talk to him about the Lord as a child. They would pray together when he stayed with her in Laguna Beach during the summers. Those memories were the happiest times in his life and the only time he heard about God. While so much of his childhood was tumultuous, he experienced peace when he was with his grandmother. Unfortunately, she died when he was in junior high, and it totally broke his heart. When he spoke of Olga, I knew Jesus was working on his heart. Where Jesus is, there is peace.

Michael and I had such a beautiful, pure love affair—nothing like anything he had ever experienced up to that point. A week into being together, he had to leave for Santa Fe for oil meetings. When I took him to the airport, I thought my life had ended. I couldn't eat, which, trust me, never happens. I cried the entire drive home from the airport. That was so not me. I once had a boyfriend tell me in college that I was about as affectionate as his dashboard. Thankfully, when he left Tulsa, Michael felt the same way and called me as soon as he landed and asked me to join him in Santa Fe. I told him I would love to come, but I would need my own room. He replied, "You can have as many rooms as you want. I just don't want to be without you." I abandoned ship in Tulsa, threw caution to the wind, and headed to Santa Fe. Two weeks into the trip, we were on a road trip when he stopped the car and said, "I am madly in love with you, and I can't live without you. Will you marry me?" I responded, "What took you so long?" To the shock of my parents, we were engaged!

We flew back to Tulsa for him to meet my parents. After dinner, my dad said, "Dru, would you and your mother excuse us? I would like to spend some time together with this fellow." I was sweating buckets. My dad always shared Christ with the guys I brought home. I didn't care if they ever called back, but I loved Michael and wanted my father to accept him. I pulled my dad aside. "Would you please take this one slow?" I asked. We had talked a lot about Jesus, but I hadn't closed the deal, so to speak. Three very long hours later, they emerged from my dad's office. I was a wreck by then. Once again, I was worried about something that I had no control over. Michael had a beautiful and emotional experience with the Lord as he asked Jesus to become the Lord of his life. We had my parent's blessing. Now, what about his family? That was quite a different story.

Let's pray together

Jesus, I thank you that You so beautifully moved on Michael s heart. And, for my behalf. Lord, I pray that every young couple comes to know You in an intimate way as they become one. Thank you for moving on people s hearts and mending lives together. Amen

Chapter 5

Becoming A Hammer

I still laugh when I think of our first Christmas together. In my family, Christmas Eve was a big time. We were corny enough that the sisters wore monogrammed matching Christmas pajamas every year. We cooked and baked most of the day, played Christmas music, and danced around the kitchen. Before dinner, my dad read us the Christmas story from the Book of Luke in the New Testament. Eventually, my mom memorized the entire Christmas story and would recite it word for word without missing a beat. After a big Christmas feast, we would go to our beautiful church for the Christmas Eve candlelight service. After the service, we put the cookies out for Santa and had hot chocolate as we talked and laughed until bedtime. I am eternally grateful for the incredible, loving home my parents made for us.

That Christmas morning, Michael and I flew out to Los Angeles so we could spend Christmas Day with his family. We pulled up to the home of his legendary and iconic grandfather, Dr. Armand Hammer. I had no idea what to expect when we walked up the big stairs to his house. We walked into the living room that was filled with Monets and Modiglianis, and there were Faberge eggs all over the house. With all these gorgeous treasures on the walls, half of them I didn't even know, I was astounded at the difference in atmosphere between this house and my parents 'house. At the gathering, there were only six of us: Armand, his wife Frances, Armand's only child Julian from his first marriage to Olga, Michael's sister, and me.

We all sat in the living room around a coffee table with an enormous tub of Russian caviar on a silver tray set. We also had Russian vodka that Armand brought back from his last trip to Russia. I never had caviar before. I was like Julia Roberts in "Pretty Woman"—minus the whole hooker thing. A piano player was playing the Steinway grand piano in a tuxedo, which struck me as odd since only six of us were there.

After talking about pleasantries, Armand rang a silver bell to summon his staff, who escorted us to the dining room. The dining room had a long table. We were seated so far apart that I couldn't even touch the person next to me. Of course, Armand and Frances were at polar ends. When he rang the bell again, a procession of people came out with huge silver platters that had huge silver domes to keep the food warm. There were more than enough for 30 people. Several men and women with black suits and white gloves with white linens draped over their arms served us. What in the world?

Thankfully, I didn't know enough about Armand to be intimidated. To me, he was just a small, cute man who stood no taller than 5'5", and he didn't seem to talk much. At that time, we couldn't look anyone up in an instant on our phones or the computer (Imagine a world before Google!), and I certainly wasn't reading the Wall Street Journal.

After the meal, he came over to my chair and asked if he could meet with me privately in his office. I was never a shy person. I thought, "No problem," as he escorted me into his office. I walked in and saw floor-to-ceiling walls of books and started laughing. I told him I had never seen a private library with the Dewey Decimal System. It struck me as so funny.

He sat me down across his desk and asked about my hobbies. I told him I had played tennis most of my life and enjoyed it. Right then and there, on Christmas Day no less, he picked up the phone and ordered someone to get me a membership at Riviera Country Club. *Now,* I was intrigued. Who was this man with the Batphone?

Then, he got serious about his only grandson. Armand wanted Michael to travel with him and learn the business from the ground up. Since there would be a lot of traveling, he wanted me to join them. "It is healthier if we stay together," he said. Finally, he got to his main request. Armand asked me if I would not work so I could travel with them around the world. Wait… not work *and* travel? Was that a trick question?

I would soon learn this meant traveling on his private 727 airplane that was like a house, staying in the finest hotels, and meeting the world's movers and shakers. Now comes the part that still makes me cringe. I turned to him and said, "Dr. Hammer, I have no problem with that request, but I have a request for you."

Can you believe that a pipsqueak right out of college would say this to Armand Hammer? I continued, "My request for you is to let me show you how to be a family." There was a long pause. Then he started laughing. "And how exactly do you propose to do that?" he asked. I told him that Sundays are family days. We go to church and then come home and have a big family supper.

"I am inviting you every Sunday that you are in town to join us for a family meal in our home." I was at least smart enough to realize that requesting he attend church with us might be a stretch to an 87-year-old Jewish man. He never answered, but he looked at me with a huge grin on his face. He didn't outright agree, but I knew he got a kick out of it.

As we left that day, we all said goodbye and Armand stood by the door and gave each of us an envelope with Oxy stock as his Christmas gift to us. As sweet of a gesture as that was, it seemed so impersonal and bizarre compared to the mounds of wrapped gifts my parents so thoughtfully chose for us three girls. Looking back, it makes me realize just how far Michael had come to being that loving father who got so much joy on Christmas with his own children.

I knew that on that first Christmas, we both had a ways to go to understand where the two of us came from. His family was so distant from each other. Everything was so formal. It was made very clear I was no longer going to live the small-town Oklahoma life anymore. The new family wasn't exactly the warm and fuzzy home I was used to. I either had to learn to adapt to the new world, or I had to jump ship. I wasn't about to do that. I was in love, and I wanted to spend the rest of my life with this funny and handsome man—my Prince Charming.

Tulsa didn't know what to do on January 12, 1985. First, there was a record freeze with a high of 12 degrees. Michael's best friends from Columbia Business School flew in to be groomsmen, including his best friend since junior high military boarding school, Larry, and his hilarious friend Tom, whom he met working at Occidental. They were all brilliant and funny, and they could party like it was 1999. I made a joke to Michael, "You party all you want and get it out of your system." He took me seriously. The night before the wedding, he and his buddies had partied all night and didn't get a wink of sleep. So, on the day of the wedding, he was so hung over that when we gave our nuptials, one eye was looking at me, and the other was straying off, looking back. Hmmm, could that have been a sign? I didn't want to give it much thought on that special day.

Armand, having bought a company City Service in Tulsa, was so excited his only grandson was getting married. He flew in a plane with loads of people and professional photographers, along with ours. Our wedding was held in the First United Methodist Church downtown. It's like St. Patrick's Cathedral in New York. It's a gorgeous cathedral you would expect to see in Europe, certainly not in Tulsa. Eight hundred people were invited, but I believe 1,000 were counted that evening. It was a scuttlebutt for that small town of 400,000. All the bridesmaids were in black velvet with thousands of red roses. The reception after the service was held downtown at the Tulsa Club. Coverage of the wedding turned up in papers around the country, and "Vanity Fair " even showed up.

Interestingly, they didn't focus on the beautiful wedding my mother had put together but on how we served Martinelli's non-alcoholic champagne. My dad was not about to conform to anyone else's lifestyle. The main picture featured in the "Vanity Fair " article was a huge silver bowl filled with iced Martinelli's sparkling apple juice. Michael's friends didn't know what to do about the beverage selection. I guarantee they had never been to a dry wedding before. They humored us as long as they could, and then they went down to the next floor's bar.

Michael was still so hungover that when we finally got back to our hotel room, both of us were completely exhausted. For me, I was so tired from trying to at least say hello to each person in attendance. We fell on the bed. Michael crashed in his tuxedo face down and didn't wake up until the next morning when it was time to leave for our flight. Quite the first night as husband and wife. Maybe another sign, but I still wasn't having it. But the lavish wedding was a sign of the beginning of a new, grandiose lifestyle.

Becoming a Hammer was a process. Armand—the Hammer patriarch—wanted me to learn the ropes fast! One of the first challenges was my wardrobe. With the three or four dinners and black-tie events I was expected to attend weekly, my college cowboy boots and broom skirts, which were the thing in those days, were not going to cut it.

The morning after coming home from our honeymoon, Michael reported to Occidental Petroleum for work. He was expected to work long hours. Even though the Hammer family was quite wealthy, money was not just handed out. Hard work was expected from all. At the time, we were living in a hotel, and my job was to find a place to live. I had no idea where I was and did not know a soul in Los Angeles. All the lives of my friends and family were going along the same, and I felt like my whole world had been turned upside down. I would sit on the edge of the bed and just cry. I didn't know what to do with myself. As glamorous as my life looked on the outside, there was a price to pay.

We were going to amazing events in the evenings, but I did not know anyone. During those days, I had nothing to do and was totally alone. Thankfully, I'm a survivor and always had the Lord to lean on. That doesn't mean it was easy. I had to learn to make my way in that crazy world.

So much of my early years with Michael was like learning on the job, not only as a mother but also as a wife. Since we had only known each other for three months, there were a lot of unknowns about each other. We knew we loved each other, and we knew we were miserable without each other. However, getting down to the nitty-gritty of daily life and how we fit together was different. For example, because he had gone through military school, he liked things in perfect order, down to making the bed a certain way. A quarter had to bounce on it. What does that even mean? I got a lesson on how to fold the corners of the sheets at the end of the bed. As he showed me, I thought, "Who puts that much time into anything so insignificant and something you're going to mess up every night?" I realized he was a clean freak. I was the messy one. A compromise was in order, which meant I just expected him to loosen up. As challenging as becoming a wife was, it pales compared to becoming a mother. Michael and I were like so many young couples in love. He wanted a big family. God knows better than anyone when the time is right. Ten months after saying "I do," I learned I was pregnant. On August 28, 1986, Michael and I welcomed Armand Douglas Hammer into the world. We called him Armie.

After Armie was born, this wonderful pediatrician, Dr. Bob, was making the rounds at UCLA and came into my room with his trusted nurse, Gerri. I was still really new in Los Angeles, and they walked in and introduced themselves to me, then asked if I would like them to pray over my baby. I almost fell to the floor. I was still very new in LA and I didn't know any other Christians. What a sign from God to send them to my hospital room.

Viktor Armand Hammer was born on June 29, 1988, almost two years after Armie.

I'm so thankful for my children. Motherhood certainly shapes your priorities. It's hard to imagine that before they came into our lives, so much of my focus was on playing the perfect Hammer wife and looking like it, too. Although I was by no means poor growing up, my parents were frugal. When I married Michael, I was not accustomed to spending a lot—especially on clothes. I was very paranoid about spending his money when we first got married.

Before saying "I do," I never relied on a man except my dad. I certainly didn't ask or expect a man to buy anything for me, but I was expected to be with him at parties and such and to look a certain way. My sweet dad kicked in and secretly sent me a clothing allowance. I also researched and found out that once a month, all the clothing designers would have sample sales on their collections. I would drive downtown and walk the floors of the designers 'showrooms. Thankfully, I was tall and thin, so I could wear the sample sizes. That process takes a lot of time, but time was something I had plenty of. I found beautiful designer clothes at 75 percent off retail prices. I was proud of myself for the bargains I got. I even got on Los Angeles" 'Best Dressed List."

My best friend Candace had just fallen in love with her now husband of 35 years, Steve Garvey. We both were going to President George H.W. Bush's inauguration in D.C. We each decided to take our finest dress. We planned to wear them at the first gala. Then, we would all meet for lunch the next day, swap dresses, and wear them for that night's gala. It's a good thing no one was looking at what I was wearing in the crowds of beautiful people that first night because Steve was hosting the second night's gala. He and Candace were up on stage with the president, and all eyes were on them. No one noticed the dress swap. My dress looked better on Candace anyway.

Candace was one of my first girlfriends I made in my new world. The way we met was such a "God thing." Michael and I had just moved into our new home in Pacific Palisades. Of course, I had the house painted a soft flesh pink with mint green shutters. Candace would take her two girls to a French school from Brentwood and pass my house every morning. She would say to herself, "That is such a happy house. I have got to meet the person who lives there." Sure enough, one day, she stopped by and rang my doorbell. I invited her in, and we immediately knew we would be lifelong friends.

Candace and I spent that morning talking about how much Jesus loved her and how He wanted to help her through a great trial. This was before she had met Steve. Right there in my living room, we knelt at my coffee table, and she asked Jesus to come into her life and help her through this difficult time. I had no idea that I, myself, would ever be in that same position someday.

She and Steve have been there for me through my own trial. Steve has escorted both of us to many parties so I wouldn't be alone. I have the privilege of being the Godmother to their son Sean. I love all their children like my own.

I was also blessed to have Michael's mother, Sue, whom I loved and adored. The two of us had become very close. I had the privilege of leading Sue to Jesus, along with her second husband. It changed her life forever. Her first husband, Julian, who was Michael's father, did not treat her well.

Sue passed away in 2010. It broke my heart. So often I have thought about how God took her home at the perfect time—one year before the collapse of our marriage. She would have been devastated if she had witnessed our divorce.

Sue would come up from San Diego at least once a month and stay a long weekend with us. She was always my safe haven. I could tell her anything. She was so proud of her son and loved being with our happy family. She seemed to be the only "normal," down-to-earth person amongst the Hammers, along with her daughter Jan and her family from her first marriage. She was a small-town girl like me. She was from Texas and understood where I was coming from. She knew the pressure of being in the Hammer family. There were a lot of perks, but that came with a lot of responsibility.

I was laughing at how Armand pulled me aside at a black-tie event and said he did not approve of the Ralph Lauren black watch plaid tuxedo I was wearing. I thought it was the coolest outfit in the world with the six-inch stilettos. It was not proper for his generation for women to wear pants at events. He didn't understand my renegade style. However, as much as I liked the look, he won. Sue and I both understood that the Hammers weren't your typical family where you drop by, make small talk, and act silly. We were the women who represented. In my new crazy life, I had to play by someone else's rules, and there were obligations, such as sometimes several black-tie events a week. It was exhausting once I had two very active sons at home. But there are no pity parties here. I experienced a life few young girls my age experienced. It taught me to grow up fast. Having a loving husband, we had an absolute blast traveling the world.

As for Armand, he did honor my request. I had to formally invite him and Frances over for Sunday supper, but he came every single Sunday when he was in town. Sometimes, we thought he would stay all day! He brought toys galore for the children, ate outside on informal plates, took naps in our backyard lounge chairs, and was gleeful just being with family. He had missed this while trying to conquer the world in his younger days. It was truly beautiful to watch, like butterflies coming to life and spreading their wings.

Little did I know that years later, I would have to spread my wings and learn to fly on my own—this time on my own terms.

Let's pray together

Jesus, You are there for us in good and tough times. People may fail us, but You will never fail us; as You said, I am the Husband to the husbandless and the Father to the fatherless." Thank you for always being faithful. Amen

Chapter 6

The Princess & The Tomboy

The people I had the privilege of meeting in my crazy new world were astounding to me. I would always ask myself, "How in the world did I end up here?" Before social events I would beg, "God, please put me next to someone who doesn't think I'm the most simple, naive person in the world." I'd also add, "God, if I can make even a smidgeon of difference in someone's life tonight, I am your girl. I will tell them about You."

I kept my word, even when I was introduced to Princess Diana. The third time I met her, I was able to share with her how Jesus loves her. The Bible says don't worry about what to say when you stand before kings—or, in my case, princesses. It says the Holy Spirit will give you the words when you need them, and that's exactly what He did for me.

For me, this first majestic meeting all happened because Armand was friends with Lord Mountbatten. He was like a father to Prince Charles. When the lord passed away, Armand became a mentor to Prince Charles, as they continued the dream of starting United World Colleges around the world. The two of them did several big fundraisers for these colleges, promoting world peace amongst students by showing leadership ability from many countries. Armand was one of the benefactors of the Armand Hammer United World College in New Mexico.

I have always said, "If you have to pay to be a VIP, then you're not a VIP." However, when it comes to royalty, everyone pays to be a VIP. One of the fundraisers was a weekend in Palm Beach full of polo matches and endless champagne. All weekend we got to ride on Armand's coattails. There were receptions of hundreds of people who got to see Prince Charles and Princess Diana, and they got a quick picture. Then, there were the VIP receptions of smaller groups of people who got to shake their hands, make small talk for two minutes, and get their picture taken—for a price, of course. Events like these cost a fortune. They are fundraisers at their finest. Because of the cost to attend, there never seemed to be many 27-year-olds present. Princess Diana and I were both in the minority in a crowd of 60, 70, and 80-year-olds. Since we both just had our first babies, we seemed to have a little bit more to talk about with each other than we did with the older people. The first time we met, we had a quick chat. Nothing more than "love the dress" and "isn't it grand to have sons?"

The next morning, Michael and I went for a long walk on the beach and stopped at a charming French bistro for breakfast. I remember thinking how sad it was that Princess Diana was living in a birdcage, although she was in the presidential suite and could have anything and everything at her disposal. She had armed guards outside her suite. She and Prince Charles could never just go out to take long walks and stop wherever they wanted for breakfast like we could. As glamorous as her life looked, she could never enjoy the simple things in life. Instead, she was on display at a zillion events, small-talking and putting on a happy face, no matter how she felt.

The second time I met Princess Diana, we were at another fundraiser with Armand and Frances in London. This time, we were taken to the country home in Balmoral. Let's just say Prince Charles loves his trees. He is a major horticulturist and is very proud of the thousands of species of trees, plants, and flowers from all over the world on his estate. And what an estate it is. He spent two hours taking a small group of us around his property. There wasn't a leaf out of place. I think he had elves that came out and picked up any leaf or twig that may have fallen off the trees.

After taking this amazing tour, our friend Al turned to Prince Charles and said, "You know, with a little money and imagination, this place could really be something." Prince Charles and the rest of us just roared in laughter. He has a great sense of humor.

Afterward, we had a beautiful lunch at their home, and Princess Diana joined us. Once again, she was thrown into a group of people she didn't know and had to chit-chat. She remembered me and asked how my sons were. We conversed about how our children were the greatest gift of our lives. Despite our friendly chatter, I could still tell she kept her guard up—and rightfully so. Many would have loved to get the big scoop from her and print it for money or simply betray her personal life for sensationalism. I totally understood her keeping conversations very surface.

The third time I saw Princess Diana was definitely God-ordained. There was a big fundraiser in Washington, D.C., for the Washington Opera. Armand was so distraught with his wife of 35 years passing he asked if Michael and I would go to D.C. and represent him.

Hmmm. Let me think about it. I may be busy… YES!

Though I had met Princess Diana before, we hadn't gone to a girl's lunch or bonded over cappuccinos. I was surprised the last time when she remembered me and addressed me by my name. I mean, she must meet tens of thousands of people. But this time, she came up to me and told me how sorry she was to hear Frances had passed away. They had spent a lot of time together, and she appreciated how wonderful Frances was to her. I, in turn, told her that when I married into the family, Frances was always so kind to me as well. I shared how I would bring the boys over, and she would sit in a chair and watch them play in her backyard. They brought her so much joy.

I am divulging this next darling story because it just shows that Princess Diana wasn't only one of the most famous and beautiful women in the world, but she also just wanted to be "one of the girls." She pulled me aside where no one could hear us talking and whispered in my ear, "No one had more incredible jewels than Frances. Did you get that gorgeous Harry Winston Burmese ruby and diamond necklace and that huge emerald, sapphire, and diamond necklace?" I burst out laughing and replied, "You have a vault of royal jewels you can choose from. The last time I saw you in Palm Beach, you wore the most incredible diamond necklace as a headband, but you remember Frances 'jewels?" She said, "No one would ever forget her jewels."

I confessed to her, "Yup, I got them! But more importantly, Frances had everything she would ever want in the world's eyes. Yet, when she died, she didn't take any of the jewels with her. They were left behind, but she had the greatest gift in the world—she had Jesus in her life as her Lord and Savior. That's the greatest treasure in life, and *that s* what she took with her."

Princess Diana just looked at me and smiled. I said all I could say before we walked back to the crowd. It was a brief moment, but God opened the door. He knows that if He opens a door, I'm walking through it. My prayer to Him had been answered.

Yes, the jewels were left to me. I tried wearing them to a few black-tie events, but I felt ridiculous. It was like I was playing 'dress up. 'Plus, in today's world, you could get your head knocked off for jewels like those. Michael and I decided to donate them to the foundation. They were sold at an auction and given to ministries.

My few times with Princess Diana were wonderful memories. That's why it made me so sad years later when I began to read the stories about her and Charles 'crumbling marriage. The press loved exploiting her frailties and how she handled her stress with an eating and emotional disorder. It is hard enough to go through an eating disorder and marital problems in private. I can only imagine what she endured, having the world read about hers.

I would never be presumptuous and say, "I know what she was going through." However, I had gone through similar things on a much smaller basis. When all the press was coming out about Princess Di's marital problems and the infidelities within their marriage, I had just been confronted with the same thing, the exact year. Public or private, no one will ever understand the complete feeling of devastation when you become aware of that kind of betrayal in your marriage unless you have personally gone through it. I pray you don't. This revelation is completely debilitating mentally, spiritually, and physically. I was broken, but at least I could grieve in private. Even my own family didn't know. Certainly, my children were kept from knowing. I had such empathy for the Princess. We were going through the same grief at the same time while having two children we were trying to protect. However, my situation wasn't all over the front page of the press.

In addition to a crippling marriage, I could relate to her in another way. Around 1980, I developed an eating disorder. At the time, no one talked about eating disorders or knew what they were. I have played tennis for most of my life. When I went to college, though, I no longer played tennis three hours a day. An obsession with my weight began in college. Except for playing intramurals amongst other sorority houses, I no longer played hours of tennis daily. However, I continued eating like I was. I packed on that "freshman 20/30." I never had a weight problem before, and it sure seemed like all the skinny girls in my sorority were getting cute dates. It didn't take a rocket scientist to figure out what to do with that information, or at least that's how I processed it.

I decided I needed to do something about it. Back when my eating disorder developed, we didn't have labels on foods. I had no idea what a carbohydrate was, much less a protein or fat gram. We all just knew if you ate too many sweets and fried foods, you would gain weight, which still seems to be pretty much the standard. I decided to take a nutrition class in college and learn more about this. The teacher made us do a brilliant experiment. He took us all to the bowling alley by the college campus. He asked us how much weight–if any–we thought we needed to lose to live a healthy life. I thought I had about 20 pounds to lose. I had to carry two 10-pound bowling balls in my backpack for two days straight. I had to carry them all the time except when I slept. My back ached, my legs were shot climbing all the hills at Oklahoma State University, and my heart raced as I walked to class. I couldn't get over the stress of 20 extra pounds put on my entire body. From that day on, I vowed I would never let myself get heavy again.

Growing up, the four food groups were chicken fried steak, ding dongs, bologna sandwiches, and chocolate icebox pie. I had to completely change how I ate, which wasn't easy in a carb-loaded sorority house. I began running. My problem is I can't "do" anything. I "overdo" everything. So, I ran and ran and ran. When I ate too much pizza with my friends the night before, I would get up early before class and run some more. I dropped 30 pounds in three months. Then, I kept thinking I was still heavy. I would look in the mirror and think I still needed to lose weight, even though I was skin and bones. Today, this is known as body dysmorphia. Thankfully, my parents called me on the carpet and told me I was getting carried away. I believe it comes down to control. Weight was something I could have complete control over. But then again, do any of us really have control over anything? Emotionally, this would mess me up when I gained a few pounds. Soon, it was all I could think about. Obsession can happen in any form—money, power, fame, etc. Anything can take your focus off of what is really important, which is our walk with the Lord. With my parents 'encouragement and God's help, I was healed from the all-consuming, excessive compulsion over body image. To this day, I'm still not overly fond of my body. Is any woman? But I try not to obsess over it. I just try to live healthy. Thinking of Princess Diana and her struggle with an eating disorder, I will say I understood what she had to deal with.

I didn't pray for Princess Diana because she was a princess. In God's eyes, she was no more important than anyone else. I always said if you have time to pray for "important people," I hope you aren't forgetting the people right next to you. The two women who worked for us for eight years, Luz and Lena, came to know the Lord, and I still pray for them all the time. Luz's son Luis, who we call George, is like a son to me and living for the Lord as well. Another couple, Berta and Noe, who worked for us for 10 years and helped raise our boys until they were grown, also came to know Jesus as their Lord through living with us. When they gave birth to their only child, the doctor told them their son Jessie had a major hole in his heart and he probably would not live.

Michael and I went to the hospital. We stood on the verse, "Whose report are you going to believe? We believe in the report of the Lord." God gave us the report that He is our healer. We laid our hands on that baby and prayed for Jessie to be completely healed and to live. Today, Jessie is a vibrant college student with a perfect heart who is madly in love with Jesus. I think he's going to be a world changer. The Lord sent these amazing people into our family to help us raise our two sons, and the Lord saved their lives by being exposed to how much He loves them. God's love compels me to love everyone in my life, regardless of their origin or status.

I continued to pray for Princess Diana, and the more I did, the more I felt her burden. For three nights, I couldn't sleep a wink. I felt like the Lord was telling me to write her a letter. Sometimes, I actually argue with God. I said, "Oh please, God, as if she would listen to me." I also thought of how embarrassing it would be to call Armand's executive assistant, Florence, and ask for Princess Diana's mailing address. Florence would think I was out of my mind. No, I'm not doing it.

Night after night, I still couldn't sleep. The idea of writing a letter to her kept gnawing at me. After a week of not sleeping, I finally said, "Okay, GOD. SHEESH." I got up at 3:00 a.m. and prayed for the Holy Spirit to write the letter for me. I sat down and wrote. I wished I had kept a copy. I don't recall what I wrote. It wasn't from me. It was from the Lord to Princess Diana, a love letter from her Father. I was just the conduit. I sucked up my pride and called Florence for the address. Florence was a remarkable woman, who we lost at 105 years old. She was loyal to the Hammer family for 60 years. She's even buried in the same cemetery. She was Armand's executive assistant for many years and the holder of the famous Rolodex.

You can imagine the look on the postmaster's face when I walked up and asked him for an overseas stamp, and then he checked where it was going to weigh for postage. I'm sure he thought I was like a child writing to Santa Claus. But I didn't care. I sent the letter. I didn't expect a response. I never got one. I did what I felt compelled to do: write to her and let her know that Jesus helped me through some similar trials and how much He loved her. I explained to her the plan of salvation was inviting Jesus into her heart and life. I also said He wants to be—and I believe He is—the only solution to her pain and loneliness. Wouldn't you know that after I popped that letter into the mail, I slept like a baby from that night on? I would never be presumptuous to say I was the only one who reached out. I believe in every person's life; the Bible says He sends people to plant, water, and grow. I'm not sure which role I played, but I do know that I had no peace until I got my lazy @$# out of bed and was obedient to what I felt He wanted me to do.

The night Princess Diana was in the tragic automobile accident, the two other men in the car were instantly killed. However, she was in a coma for hours before she passed away. I truly believe God kept her alive because she had heard the truth from me and others, and He gave her the gift of time in the end to reach up. God doesn't just do that for princesses. He will move mountains for all who call out His name. The world lost a princess, but the biggest tragedy is that her two sons lost their mother. And motherhood seemed to be the most important thing in the world to Princess Diana.

Sometimes it's hard to understand why things happen. Why was her life cut short like so many others? But what I do understand is the Lord turns bad into good, and everything will be justified in the end. This world isn't fair. That's why we must hang on for dear life until it's all fair in heaven with our Savior. It's a lesson I would be reminded of time and time again.

Let's pray together

Jesus, I am so grateful for everything You have blessed me with. Thank you for teaching me that life is not about material things but sharing You with others. When I am not smart enough, sophisticated enough for the world, You give me the words to speak to people who need Your love… and that, to me, is the greater meaning of life. I m so grateful, Lord. Amen

Chapter 7

The Glass Slipper

Life offers a lot of serendipitous experiences. Meeting the Princess was just one of many. I can't help but recall one of Armand's huge birthday bashes. Everyone from political figures like the president of Russia, Mikhail Gorbachev, and the president of France, Francois Mitterrand, to movie stars like Gregory Peck, Jimmy Stewart, and Cary Grant attended. Even famous rabbis were in attendance. I thought I had died and gone to heaven.

I wasn't cool enough to even pretend in front of these people that it wasn't a big deal to a small-town girl like me. I was so grateful there were no cell phones then. Back then, I wouldn't have had the maturity not to take those photo ops, which would have embarrassed the entire family. I totally would have framed all my pictures with them all over the house.

Speaking of celebrities, one time, Michael and I were flying on Armand's plane to a charity event. The legendary columnist Pauline Phillips, also known as Abigail Van Buren of Dear Abby, and her sweet husband, Morton, were on the plane with us. She sat next to me and told me she loved the dress I had worn the night before and asked where I purchased it. I was so excited to tell her that I bought it at a sample sale and that people could go downtown and hit the designer showrooms and buy the samples. She remarked, "That must take a lot of time." I told her, "Yes, but well worth the time, as you get the dresses 75 percent off."

I still laugh today at her fabulous, honest answer. She replied, "Honey, I have a lot more money than I have time."

Now, back to Armand's birthday event I had mentioned. I needed glass slippers desperately living my Cinderella fairy tale. With the party approaching, I headed downtown to try to find an evening gown. After buying the gown, my next outing was to look for appropriate black-tie shoes. I couldn't believe how expensive they were. Much to my dismay, there are no sample shoes in a size 10. As a matter of fact, no shoe looks great in that size. My dad would laughingly say, "She has a good understanding."

After spending money on a dress, I couldn't imagine spending that kind of money on one pair of shoes. I had a "lightbulb" moment. I can work this system like I have in the past. I went down to one of those shoe stores where you dye shoes to match your outfit for weddings and such. But oh no, I didn't stop there. I knew I could make those shoes even fancier. I headed to a craft store and bought glue and glitter—somebody stop the madness! On the day of the birthday bash, I was out on our balcony spraying glue on those babies and then pouring glitter on them. Now, when I see Cristian Louboutin shoes, I realize I was 35 years ahead of the curve of glitter shoes. But there was just one difference, I didn't think through the whole process as well as Louboutin.

While I was out on the dance floor that evening, I noticed I was leaving trails of glitter wherever I went. By the end of the night, dancing and thinking, "I was all that," I had huge bald spots on my shoes where they rubbed together. Michael said he could always find me that night because he simply followed the glitter.

I was so enamored with all the famous people I kept thinking, "Lord, what in the world am I doing in this big Hammer world?" You want the surprising truth? I must confess I was so unsophisticated. Initially, I thought my husband's grandfather, Armand Hammer, was the Arm and Hammer baking soda, and he did something in the oil business on the side. Back then, there was no internet to look these people up. I felt I had nothing to offer world changers and sophisticated people.

Then, I had an aha moment at one of those black-tie dinners that changed my perspective forever. I was seated next to the sweetest 88-year-old man, who was in a wheelchair. I, of course, had no idea who he was. I began my usual small talk. As I introduced myself, he was so dear to say, "I know all about you. Armand has raved about what a ray of sunshine you are in the family." I was really touched by that because I didn't know what he thought of me at the time. Then, the gentleman introduced himself. "Hello, I'm James Roosevelt." He was the oldest son of President Franklin D. Roosevelt. What a humble, kind man he was. I was so taken by his humility and grace that I was compelled to hear his story. When I heard he fought in World War II, he immediately became my hero, not because he was a president's son, but because, being born into privilege, he still left all the comforts of that life and fought for our country's freedom. As all military men and women do, he was willing to lay down his life so that we Americans can live freely in this great country. I get very mushy when it comes to service men and women. I cry in airports and run up to tell our military service how much I appreciate them for sacrificing everything for our country. I later found out that Mr. Roosevelt had received the Navy Cross for extraordinary heroism while serving as a Marine Corps officer during the war. He never mentioned that to me in our conversation. He only said that he served. Now *that* is humility.

After speaking with Mr. Roosevelt for a while, he asked me how I met Armand's grandson, being that I'm from Tulsa. I began telling him my story of growing up in such a wonderful, Godly home. My home may have seemed insignificant in the world's eyes, but my parents taught me to love Jesus and to always put God first. It's because of that, I met my husband while flying on an airplane. (And maybe because my parents prayed their entire lives for the right, Godly mate for their three daughters.) As I simply shared how I learned to love Jesus, I looked at him and noticed a tear running down his face. He took my hand and told me that his father was running for president when he was a young man in his twenties. In those days, they campaigned from town to town on trains. Every town they went to, James and his father would kneel while on the train and pray for God's guidance and favor with the people before they headed out to give speeches. When the news announced that his father had won the presidency, FDR said, "Now, son, we need to kneel down in the Oval Office and thank the Lord for answering our prayers." He told me they thanked the Lord for giving their family the opportunity and asked God to guide them. As he told me this, more tears started rushing down his face. He said, "I haven't thought about this story in over 40 years. You have inspired me to start thinking more about God in my later years. Thank you." I prayed for him right there at the table.

I was right. I didn't have anything to offer these important people. God did. No matter who or where people are in their lives, Jesus says He loves us so much that He "leaves the 99 sheep to go after the one lost sheep." (Luke 15:4) He put me next to Mr. Roosevelt so he could hear and remember how much God loves him and to remind him of those wonderful memories praying to God with his father.

Jesus went after that "one sheep" at the gala. That simple conversation changed my perspective of having to look right on the outside. My insecurity about not living up to these high-class standards suddenly melted away after meeting Mr. Roosevelt. I kept questioning God. What in the world am I doing in this life in Los Angeles? Isn't it amazing how we tell God what's right or wrong? I don't fit in. I'm not smart enough. I don't dress well enough. I'm not a blue blood. But right at that moment with Mr. Roosevelt, I realized something. He didn't care about how smart I was, what I was wearing, or what family I came from. In the last 50 years, no one else had apparently spoken to him about how much God loved him, which sparked all those beautiful memories of him and his father kneeling to thank God.

My philosophy on fashion changed from that day forward. I bet if you asked any woman (or man, for that matter) who won the Academy Award last year and what they were wearing, you would be hard-pressed to get the answer. Even if they had been on every magazine cover. So why in the world would anyone even care or remember what I wear? Having lived in Beverly Hills and Bel Air for a quarter of a century, I've learned a lot about fashion and design. After all, I had to become a quick study. And you know what, I can still travel for two weeks with only a carry-on. To this day, I'm not extravagant. Now, if Tom Ford wants to dress me as he has my son, I'd be willing to add a hanging bag to my usual carry-on when traveling. Oh, but I must have room for the glass slippers.

Let's pray together

Jesus, I know that what You desire is to have a relationship with all of us, whether we are princesses or commoners. You love all of us equally. Thank you for dying on the cross and sacrificing all so we can spend an eternity with You. How could I ever be grateful enough for everything You have done for us? Amen

Chapter 8

The Accidental Career

When Michael and I first married, we got off the plane from our honeymoon in Las Brisas resort in Mexico and moved straight to Los Angeles. We moved into a hotel first, and my job was house hunting. I didn't know where Sunset Blvd was. I had to drive and drive and drive all around with my Thomas Guide (that's dating myself!) with all the street maps until I found affordable places in Los Angeles. You couldn't buy a garage in Los Angeles for what a whole house in Tulsa cost. I couldn't believe it.

Our wonderful realtor, Paul, found a home on Rossmore Drive, just barely making it into Bel Air. We purchased the home for $327,000. Armand and my dad paid for half of the purchase, and we took out a loan on the other half. The house was adorable, but the surfaces were dated, at least as far as I was concerned. I had no idea what I was doing, but I knew I wanted to replace all the tiles in the kitchen and redo the bathrooms. I had the "ingenious idea" of going down to the lumber yard to get a few illegal immigrants to tear everything out. I knew it wasn't the best idea, but they would happily work. I mean, what could possibly go wrong? In my horrible, broken Spanglish, I said, "Afueta por favor," pointing to all the mauve-colored tiles. I hoped that registered as, "Take all the tiles out, please." Michael said to leave the house and just let them do the work. Well, when I came back, not only were all the tiles ripped out in the kitchen and master bath, but the cabinets, walls, and everything else were ripped out. I came back to nothing but 2x4's behind the walls. I guess I missed something in the translation!

I had more money than Michael when we purchased the first home because I was a saver. I had my own business in Tulsa after college, and my dad purchased a darling house for me there when I graduated. He made a deal with me that I could keep any profits on it when I sold. I painted rooms myself and bought darling furniture. I like to say I "lipsticked it." I made a $56,000 net profit, which was a lot of money for that time, as a side gig. I was able to buy all the furnishings and do most of the work for the new home in Bel Air.

That first home had a pool right off all the glass doors on the back of the house. When I was pregnant, I remember being hesitant about bringing up children in that home. (You think differently when a child is coming into your life). This home only had two bedrooms, and we were growing as a family and had grandparents coming in to visit. We needed an extra bedroom. After sprucing it up a bit, I figured we could make a profit if we put it on the market.

Michael's family knew an older couple who lived in the Huntington Palisades, which is very desirable for families. Evelyn and Ann were a lesbian couple. I lived under a rock—I had never met a lesbian couple, at least not that I knew of. I absolutely fell in love with them, and they fell in love with our growing family. Nothing made them happier than when I would bring Armie over to play. The Palisades has a small-town feel. There are parks and mom-and-pop stores; you can walk anywhere in town. The two women needed to sell and move into an independent living facility. We could purchase their home directly, a total "God thing." However, the house needed everything. It had not been touched in 40 years. We moved into an apartment in Westwood for eight months while we gutted the house. This time, still flying by the seat of my pants, was the first time I needed permits and a general contractor. I drew up the plans on pieces of paper. Well, I found a draftsman to "put it on paper" to get it ready to submit for city permits. So much to learn! I extended the kitchen and added a master bath and big closets. I redid the other baths, too. I must say, I really spiffed up the entire house. I painted the outside a real pale pink with light, mint green shutters. Why not? We purchased the home for $425,000 and put around $200,000 into it. We loved it, and Luz, who to this day is part of our family, had just come to work for us. Viktor was born in that house. We had two wonderful years living in that home. In 1988, housing prices were booming. This time, I was curious to see what kind of profit we could make instead of moving for more space. We put that home on the market. It sold for $1,150,000. I thought we had hit the motherload! With that sale, a career was "accidentally" started. Well, God ordained it. I knew we would miss the small-town feel in the Palisades, but I knew I wouldn't miss the ocean fog that loomed over that town. Many months when it was gorgeous and sunny further east, it was "June gloom" in the Palisades. Cold and damp. I was so blessed to have my two-year-old and my newborn, an incredible relationship with my husband, many new neighborhood friends, and a wonderful church, The Light House. I marveled at how good God was to me.

When the house in the Palisades sold, I found a home in Brentwood. It was a darling English cottage, much larger for our family. We purchased that home, and again, I changed it up. I extended the kitchen and master suite. This was not just to redesign. I learned you sell a house to a woman 90 percent of the time, and they like big, open kitchens and large master baths and closets. This was the home that Armand and Francis would come to every Sunday when they were in town. That is where I started ministering to them, buying them Bibles, and subtly speaking to them about the love of God. I thought I had the perfect life there. I even had Bible studies once a week, and over 100 women came.

At the time, we couldn't afford to rent something and pay for construction on this Brentwood home, plus a mortgage. All our profits from the Palisades home had to go toward purchasing the new house and the deeper construction project. At least I knew more of what I was doing at this point. We decided to bite the bullet, move in, and live through the construction. So, for eight months, it was crazy busy. I was raising two young sons while being surrounded by construction. I knew exactly what I wanted to add to this house. This time, I thought I was an architect. I went and got draft paper, rulers, and stencils. I went to town. I had the entire house planned out on crumpled pieces of paper. Planning that house became my entertainment at night. I would stay up in the middle of the night, pouring over magazines and working on dimensions. I didn't know it then, but God was creating the ability to see spaces and designs when I walked into a room. I would have been ten times more dangerous if I had the internet back then and the ability to order online. Without that luxury, I dragged my sons to plumbing fixture stores, lumber yards, light fixtures stores, and more. They didn't seem to mind and took many naps while I wheeled them around in their strollers. For eight months, we lived in a filthy construction site. We lived in two original bedrooms and switched around which bathrooms we could use. A refrigerator was even plugged in in one of the bedrooms. Looking back, I don't know how I didn't go mad. But crazy enough, I absolutely loved the chaos and watching my creation come to fruition. I had two friends, Sally and Peggy. We all had children the same age. We would take the children to the beach clubs and wear them out before bed. Michael's grandfather had died during that time, and Michael was rarely home at dinner time. Meanwhile, Peggy's husband was a restaurateur and was at their restaurants in the evenings. And Sally's husband was a workaholic. We were the Three Stooges, inseparable in raising our children together. That house became a home.

It was during this time I found out that Michael was having affairs. Then, the home reverted right back to a house, and it was the most unhappy time of my life. I truly thought we had it all before that. It's amazing how situations can change in a second. But, if I'm being honest with myself, I knew something was up because Michael would come home later than just "working late." I was crushed when I found out. This is where forgiveness played a pinnacle role in the following 19 more years of marriage, which I will get into. But for now, we decided we would leave California. The high taxes may have been the catalyst, but frankly, I needed a new start and needed to be surrounded by my family, even though it was never spoken about. We both decided Dallas would be the perfect place to raise our boys, and my sisters and their families lived there. Highland Park is the quintessential family town. The kind with Fourth of July parades, and horse and carriage rides at Christmas. Dallas is a sophisticated city with a small-town feel.

I fell in love with Texas. I still have very dear friends today from the four years we lived there. I could've stayed in Texas with my family for the rest of my life. Plus, I did my dream home there. It was a magnificent Italianate limestone home built in the 1930s by the famed architect Hal Thomson. I learned quickly in my career that good architecture is the key. Then, restore versus renovate. You keep the "rhythm," if you will. Then, a wonderful jewel box emerges. This home had a double lot that could double the size of the house, with six-car garages and beautiful living quarters and playrooms above. I still drive by the house every time I'm in Dallas and I think how fortunate I was to be able to do that home when I was only 29 years old. And you know what, I would do the same thing today even with all my many more years of experience. I would chalk that up to a great architect and the Lord, as "all good gifts come from above."

Michael had an itch to move to the Cayman Islands (supposedly, there are even better tax breaks there than in Texas), and he always fantasized about raising children in the Caribbean. He kept begging me to go to the island and look for property. I thought this was a faze and he would get it out of his system. He didn't. The next thing I knew, Michael wanted to go down there and check out the real estate. I told him to go and let me know his thoughts. He flew down and called me that night and said, "You better come down here because I am about to buy some large lots in a new development called "Vista del Mar" by the Yacht Club. He added that I could build some fabulous homes down there. Clever.

I got on a plane to go look at the lots he was about to purchase. And purchase he (we) did. Starting from scratch, I began building a 10,000-square-foot Mediterranean home on a cliff overlooking the gorgeous Caribbean Ocean. We once again had to move to a condo temporarily. Our new place took almost two years to build. Back then, 30 years ago, there were no lumber yards in the Cayman Islands. I had to work with our contractor from Dallas, who had years of experience in building. His name was Bob, and we loved him and his wife. This was a whole other level than my previous ventures. We had to import everything, right down to the nails. There was also a completely different island culture to learn. I'm laid-back, but I also like to get my hands dirty and get things done. I had to learn to not be in any hurry. I was not going to change the islander's mentality. I was the one who would have to adjust. While I missed my extended family and friends, I stayed busy building two large homes there and starting a Christian school. Grace Christian Academy is still going strong down there. There was not a good Christian school on the island at that time. After importing everything for a large house project, starting a school didn't seem to be that daunting. I figured I could either complain about not having a good Christian school for my sons or do something about it.

I went on a search for the perfect property for a small school for my sons and other island families wanting the same thing. I found a little bed and breakfast with eight-bedroom suites. How perfect that each classroom had its own bathroom. The lobby served as the entrance and principal's office. I flew to Tulsa, hired consultants in the education curriculum, and interviewed Oral Roberts University grads in the education department. If I was going to do this, I wanted the school to have the best curriculum and confirm everything we were teaching our children was the way of the Lord. Of course, I painted each room a crazy Caribbean color. My dear friend Ingrid jumped right in and even split the renovation cost. Now, that is a friend and a sign from God that I was on the right road.

In the first year, we started with eight students. Today, it's a darling, thriving school with seven other buildings added to the original. I was asked to speak at the school a few summers ago. They had graduates come back and share how the school saved their lives. Nothing is better or more important than that. Now, the school goes through high school, and many surrounding lots have been purchased for more buildings.

I ended up selling our 10,000-square-foot home in the Caymans to a shipping magnate, making around $2.5 million in profits. I also built another home in that development as a speck house that was around 6,000 square feet.

We moved back to the States. We sold homes and bought the building on 57th Street in NYC, where Hammer Galleries had rented for 27 years. I begged Michael to look into buying that beautiful six-story building on one of the widest and busiest streets. We purchased the building in New York for $6.5 million and a home in Santa Monica for $1.4 million. Years later, Michael sold that building for $27 million. We were offered $35 million from George Soros while we were under contract. Neither of us felt it was right not to honor the contract we already had in hand. Who knew who George Soros was back then! All these profits had nothing to do with me. I just showed up, rolled my sleeves up, and went to work as I learned from people much smarter than me. I also learned what not to do over all those years. I know God knew my future. Because of documents I was unaware I had signed— lesson learned—I had signed away my life. If I had not done 27 properties during my marriage and made large profits, I would have come out of it penniless. Since this does happen to many women, my goal is to keep working and help other women. You can only understand the devastation of betrayal, emotionally and financially, unless you have gone through it. I empathize with these women and am out to change the world Jesus has placed me in. Since 1985, I have been honing my skills so I can do just that.

I felt like living back in Los Angeles was the Lord guiding us. At the time, Armie was having a rough and sad time. I questioned if I missed a message from the Lord. Then his acting career took off, and he would have had to be in Hollywood for that. Viktor was happy there, so everything seemed to work out.

We bought a condo in Brentwood while gutting a gorgeous 1926 Mediterranean home with the most beautiful bones in the world. It had a huge limestone staircase in the middle of the house. Four bedrooms had balconies that overlooked the living room with large arched doorways and French doors throughout. It was truly spectacular. We got this home so inexpensively in L.A. because it needed everything—electrical work, new plumbing, and every bath, kitchen, and more had to be gutted. We added a pool and underground parking. We purchased it for $1.4 million and put $1.6 million into the house. A few years later, it sold for $7.2 million. I only include a few of these housing prices to reiterate how the Lord blessed my business beyond anything I could have done on my own. We moved and uprooted our family countless times and lived in tiny quarters or filthy construction sights for years. We tried to make it a fun adventure for the boys.

From there, we bought a 15,000-square-foot home in Brentwood. It had everything, even a professional movie theater with velvet curtains, a stage, a wine room, four loft bedroom suites, on and on. Truly out of this world. Yet, other buyers couldn't look past the distasteful decorating and finishes. Not that I'm a design genius, but by then, I had a lot of practice and a lot of studying of the different styles and how to decorate to suit different architectural styles. I renovated all the surfaces and brought them up to date. We had an amazing couple, Berta and Noe, who lived with us for years and helped keep up that large house. I didn't particularly want that large of a house, but it was never about what I wanted or needed. It was solely about how much money I could make on the homes after renovating. I was never emotional about any of the homes. They were all beautiful, and I loved living in every one of them. But when I was done with the work and settled, I was on a mad search for my next project. It was fun, but by then, I considered it my "job." I was addicted to the chase of my next project. It became very apparent that my sons would never be raised in the conventional way where you grow up in the same family home and neighborhood. Did it maybe damage them from moving so much? I'd like to think it "expanded them," as they are the most independent young men in the world. They adapt to any environment. This, especially for Armie, has come in handy, living on movie sets and weeks on the road all over the world promoting his work. Even Viktor and his wife have moved around and always settled well. Wherever they go, they always find wonderful friends and churches.

After selling that home in Brentwood, we purchased the beautiful English Tudor estate right across the street from the Bel Air Hotel on Stone Canyon. We bought the home from the great NBA player and coach KikI VanDeWeghe. Again, the bones were gorgeous, but it needed updating. The pro was a creek that ran under a bridge into the Bel Air Hotel Pond on the picturesque grounds, where the famous white swans swam as you entered. Several times, I got phone calls from the manager saying, "Mrs. Hammer, your black lab is chasing our swans again today. Can you please come and get her?" This house was also the home of the famous actress Greer Garson. She lived there for many years next door to Janet Leigh, who still lived there when we purchased the home. It was so beautiful, with library paneling throughout and linenfold wood-carved walls in the dining room. There was even a hidden prohibition room in the library paneling where the butler would hand out alcoholic drinks to the guests. We lived in the staff quarters for a year as the home was being totally renovated and every bath and kitchen completely restored. My sons still laugh about how we had this tiny staff kitchen with a little microwave, a toaster oven, and half a refrigerator for over a year. It just shows you how little you really need in life. The one and only Charles Faudre', a designer out of Tulsa and publisher of nine incredible design books, worked with me on interior designs. I think one reason I loved getting new design projects was an excuse to work with him. We did four houses together. By then, I stopped saying, "I love this house. I'm going to stay in this one forever."

One day, a man came whisking in to see the house with his fiancé, both in matching Porsches with paper tags. She, of course, was a gorgeous blonde. I asked the couple when they were getting married, and they replied in a month. This clearly wasn't his first marriage. When they left, I told Michael, "If they want this house, he will want a quick close."

Sure enough, he wanted a 20-day closing. That meant I was on the hunt for a new place. A new project! I poured over the real estate section every day. I am really dangerous now since Zillow and realtor.com are available. I will stay up until the middle of the night and know pretty much every property on the market in the city I live in and the listings in my other favorite cities.

There was a stunning home on what I think is the greatest street in Santa Monica, La Mesa. It was an ultra-contemporary home that I had kept my eyes on for months. Here's a little secret: I only buy homes that have been on the market for a long time. That offers more flexibility on the price. I always try to buy houses at a good value. I want the houses that need everything and the ones most people are afraid to tackle. I knew this house's profit margin would be great since it overlooked the gorgeous Riviera Country Club. Funny enough, that was the country club where Armand got me the membership on the first Christmas I met him. The view was absolutely spectacular.

After the offer came in on our home, I went to see this contemporary jewel box. This home used to be the home of Lee Radziwill, socialite and sister of Jackie Kennedy. The master bath was the chicest bathroom I had ever seen and was way too good for me to design. The living room, master bedroom, and kitchen had floor-to-ceiling sliding glass doors that slid into the walls to become an indoor/outdoor feeling onto a huge patio that was directly across from the Riviera Clubhouse. It took my breath away. What fun I had with this home. I had never done a contemporary before. I still drive by that house when I'm in town. It doesn't look like much from the outside, but when you walk in, it's stunning. When I went to see this house, I walked into one of the upstairs bedrooms and saw this picture of the son with his dad, and I thought to myself, "That man looks so familiar." Surely enough, this home was the family home, before a divorce, of the man who was in escrow on our home in Bel Air! So, we basically switched homes. You seriously couldn't write it any better in a city of nearly four million people!

I woke up every morning enchanted by this home. I loved living in that sexy, contemporary home. While having coffee outside one morning on that gorgeous patio, as I was overlooking the beautiful view, I prayed. I said aloud, "God, if You ever want me to sell this home, then You'll have to bring a buyer to our doorstep." Wouldn't you know it, three months later, a note was left on our front door. It was from a woman who wrote, "This may be crazy, but my husband plays golf at Riviera, and every time he tees off in front of your house, he comes home and says he would love to buy it. If you would ever be interested in selling, would you please give us the first option?" Obviously, she didn't know who she was talking to! We soon had the nice couple over for a glass of wine and a charcuterie plate. After pleasantries, the men went out on the patio and made a deal. After they agreed on the price, Michael asked what he did. He explained that he basically invented saccharin and the pink packets are his company along with the sugar in the raw brown packets and several others. Michael said, "Well, if I had known that, I would have asked for more!" We made a great profit. Both parties were thrilled. That gorgeous home recently sold for $18 million. In this line of work, you can't look back. You just keep moving forward and making profits. I always prayed over the homes and told the buyers that these homes were blessed. I wanted to share the love of Jesus with buyers and left beautiful Bibles with their names inscribed on them. What buyers didn't know was that when the homes were under construction, I would always write Bible verses in big black markers before floors were laid and drywall was installed.

After we sold that home, we purchased the Henry Mancini home in Holmby Hills. It was a beautiful country French home that Henry and his wife Jenny had built. It looked like a 1920s French Villa in the middle of the city, but it was completely hidden behind large stone walls and Ficus trees. There was a giant living area with three rooms and the most gorgeous wood ceilings and fireplaces. In the kitchen I did the stoves and all the cabinetry in the French la Cornue. The stoves had all these fancy burners for the "chef extraordinaire," which I basically purchased for the looks. I have no idea or desire to create fancy dinners. The upstairs office was one of my favorite rooms in the house. Mr. Mancini wallpapered the walls in his original sheet music. There was "The Pink Panther," "Moon River" and hundreds more. After an extensive renovation, we put the home on the market. We purchased that home for $5.2 million and put around $2 million into it. We listed it on the market and sold it for $15.5 million. It was a score, not because we made a wonderful profit, but what we were able to do with the profit.

Kelsey Grammar and his wife at the time came to look at the home and fell in love with it. It certainly helped that Kelsey was a huge Mancini fan. They immediately put in an offer, and we came up with a fair value for the market and the special house it was. While in escrow, the Grammars had a leak in their home in Malibu while they were out of town. When they returned, they found the entire downstairs was completely flooded. We received a call from the realtor saying they were not able to close since they had to deal with fixing their Malibu home. Michael and I prayed about it, and we felt like we should give them back their deposit even though the down payment was issued and contingencies were released. However, we had our realtor call them and let them know we were sending them back their down payment. A year later, Kelsey and his wife fixed and sold their home in Malibu, and Kelsey could not get our home off his mind. Kelsey had his realtor call ours. We had taken the house off the market while working on another house. The Grammars wanted to come back and see the house again. I let their realtor know we would happily let them see the house, but I would be there to visit with them to discuss. At that time, real estate in Los Angeles had increased 10 percent from the previous year. When Kelsey and his wife came over, I explained that if they wanted the house, it would cost them more–a million dollars more. I wasn't asking that for self-gain. By that time, I was able to gift a million dollars from each house I renovated. This time, I asked Kelsey to match my million to the Dream Center in Los Angeles, an organization I had become very involved with years before. I explained to Kelsey what the center does for those reclaiming their lives after abuse and addiction. The Dream Center says they don't "rehabilitate," they "restore." They restore lives back to Jesus. As I was doing so, he had tears running down his face. He explained how the loss in his own family led him into years of addiction. You could tell Kelsey had a heart for God. He happily took my deal. When I look back at times like that, I see the pieces of the master puzzle. In one short year, the Lord took a million-dollar donation and changed it to two million for the Dream Center. It cost one million dollars to renovate an entire floor for hurting people at that time. Now, two floors provide a safe haven so people will be restored. That's a big hallelujah!

As I mentioned, I poured over the real estate sections every day. And I definitely lived for the thick Sunday edition! I knew there was this one home in Pasadena that was the most exquisite home I've ever seen. (I feel like I always say that!) The home was built in 1927. The gentleman who built it was raised very poor in England, and when he was 12 years old, he was a stowaway on a ship to the United States. And I thought I had guts! He came with nothing but was scrappy enough to get to Los Angeles. He became one of the largest landowners in California through sheer determination to succeed. He saw an English manor as a child in the late 1800's. He would ride his bicycle by this manor and would say to himself, "I am going to go to America and make millions, and I am going to copy this house exactly and build it in California." Well, that is exactly what he did in 1927. He hired the best architect in California, maybe in all of America. Paul Williams, the first African American member of the American Institute of Architects, designed this home. In my opinion, his homes are the epitome of low-key style and class. Mr. Atkins purchased the perfect five acres that overlooked the beautiful bridge entering Pasadena, right on San Rafael Drive. He hired Mr. Williams, and the first thing he did was send him to England to copy as closely as possible the countryside manor in England he loved as a child. Mr. Atkins wanted the same iron manufacturing company for all the iron railings and light fixtures, wood carving company, stone masons, stained glass designers, etc. Mr. Williams returned from a six-week journey of tracking down all the craftsmen of the original home. He sat down with Mr. Atkins and said he had good and bad news for him. "The good news is I located and hired all the craftsmen that built the beautiful English Tudor and Gothic revival style home you grew up loving. The bad news is this will cost you over $300,000 to build." While waiting for a response, the owner replied, "The huge homes in Montecito cost $500,000 to build, so I want you to go up there and meet with the prolific architect George Washington Smith and see what special things they are doing in those homes. I got to experience the results of that partnership. When I went to look at the home 88 years later, I couldn't believe that even down in the "Batcave" basement, there were exquisite stained-glass windows of depictions of the owner with his friends playing cards, shooting pool, and hunting. The basement had gorgeous carved beams that were just as beautiful as the ones on the main floors. There were inlaid marble floors, a hand-carved bar, a Roman-style spa, and so much more. Mr. Williams certainly figured out ways to spend the extra $200,000, which may not have been easy to do when an average family home in Pasadena cost $30,000 to build then. Now, right in front of me to purchase was a 17,000 square foot home with 10 bedrooms, eight baths, a carriage house with eight stalls for horses, which was converted to a guest house and horsepower. That worked perfectly for a husband who was obsessed with cars.

After laboring for 14 months to bring this magnificent home back to its grandeur, it burned to the ground two weeks before we were to move in. Armie and I had surprised my parents in Budapest for one of my father's healing and ministry services. We had flown home, and Michael and Viktor picked us up from the airport. We all went straight to dinner. Immediately, we heard from our neighbor, Gale Anne Hurd, ex-wife of James Cameron and a prolific producer in her own right. She had become a friend of mine during the months of construction. She called and asked, "Have you seen the news?" I told her we just got back into the country. "Well, I really hate to be the one telling you this, but your house is on fire." When we hung up, I kept thinking there must be a mistake. The four of us hopped in the car and drove to the house. I still was in doubt. When we got a few miles away, we saw fire spewing 100 feet in the air. There was so much toiling, but my biggest disappointment was that the home could never be replaced. That kind of craftsmanship can't be duplicated.

Suspiciously, another home in Brentwood, around the corner from the house I renovated, had also burned just a few weeks before their move-in day. It was ruled arson. Only one sub-contractor worked on both homes, and the exact same chemicals had been used. He very calculatingly poured the inflammable oil, starting from the top floor, down the stairs into the basement, making sure the house wouldn't just burn but smash to the ground. By the time we arrived, the roof had crashed two floors down, obliterating the entire house. There was nothing to salvage from the house.

The four of us stood there in shock, not saying a word to each other, nor did all the firefighters, realizing there was nothing they could do. We were so grateful for the brave men who tried their hardest to save our home.

After our home burned, the fire chief came to interview us and Armie, who was living in the guest house at the time. We were immediately ruled out as suspects. The chief informed us that only around 14 percent of arsons are found because most of the evidence is burned. When they interviewed the one subcontractor who worked on both homes that burned, he failed the lie detector test, but you can't make a conviction on that test. We were so confused as to why anyone would do such a thing, but the chief bluntly said that sometimes people are just envious of what others have. For some, it's even sexually arousing to watch a place burn. Go figure that!

I know that home was just a material "thing," but I had worked so painstakingly hard on that beautiful home. In the scheme of life, we were healthy and thankful none of us were injured or killed in that fire. I must admit, though, I did have a pity party for a while over the loss of the most beautiful home I have ever had.

The beautiful thing that came out of that project was my new-found friend. When we were in escrow on that house, I asked the sellers if I could come over and spend a little time with our contractor. When I drove into the gate, I noticed an older man in his late 80's sitting on one of the stone benches on the grounds. When the owner let me in, she said to me, "When you move into this house, there is an older gentleman who comes with the house." At 17, he became Mr. Atkins 'chauffeur and drove for him until he passed away. He lived in the carriage house and devoted his life to caring for the owner. He never married or had children. He would come over and piddle in the yard. He just enjoyed being on the property. I couldn't believe how dear that story was. When I was leaving, I walked down and introduced myself. I immediately fell in love with him. His name was Ralph. I assured him that I would restore the house to its original grandeur, and he was always welcome to come inside and watch all the progress and help himself to anything. He started choking up, which, of course, made me choke up. I wish I could write even more chapters to tell all the wonderful stories he told me about the owner, not to mention how he added to my life.

He told me how Mr. Atkins owned not only many buildings downtown but also the racetracks in Los Angeles and Tia Juana. He also owned the ranch where the famous Seabiscuit horse lived and trained. I loved hearing about all the famous people he entertained and hobnobbed with, like Charlie Chaplin, using that secret prohibition closet at parties. I would call Ralph and let him know when I was on my way to the home. I would always find him waiting for me on the stone bench. After looking at the progress on the home, we would go to lunch together. A year into our friendship, I received a call informing me Ralph had passed away. I was heartbroken. Ralph was a very quiet, shy man, and he loved God. I have always thought about how Ralph got to see his home that he was so sentimental about being restored. I am grateful he didn't see that home burn to the ground. He passed away just a month before. God's timing is always perfect. My big takeaway from that tragedy is I got to know Ralph, and I believe I gave him joy in the last year of his life. I know he gave me joy. We made other special friends from Pasadena. One was Martha Williamson, who created the television show "Touched by an Angel." I believe that program touched millions of people's lives and made Jesus relatable. Her husband, John, was wonderful, too.

After that devastation from the house we lost, we bought a gorgeous Hollywood regency-style home in Beverly Hills at 1150 Tower Road. It was designed by famed architect Wallace Neff, who had built some of the most beautiful homes in Los Angeles. Mr. Neff was famous for his oval-shaped entrances with curved 10-foot doors leading into all the rooms. I totally gutted this home, tripled the size of the kitchen, and added a large den off the kitchen. It had a view of all of Beverly Hills directly behind the Beverly Hills Hotel. On one trip to Europe, I found these hand-carved, enormous antique bookshelves at an auction. They had come out of a chateau in the south of France. I can't even imagine how much they must have weighed. They were 11 feet high and 13 feet wide. We bought them and had them shipped over. At the time, we didn't have a place for them. We hoped someday we would find one. They had been in storage for years. One day, Michael came home and said, "Dru, we have been storing these for so long. We either need to use them or sell them." Let's just say that was a big mistake on his part. The next day, I went to the new house and had the architect meet me there with the builder. I told them there would be a change in the kitchen plans. I ultimately doubled the size of the kitchen to accommodate the huge bookshelves, which would now be used as kitchen cabinets. I then had a 10x10 center aisle built with the cabinet doors below carved to match the beautiful linen fold on the antique bookshelves. It was a masterpiece—not because of me, but because of those darn antique bookshelves I finally got to use!

With the nudge of our realtor, Drew, he suggested buying the home next door. It was a wonderful family home, and most importantly, it could be purchased at a great price since it needed a good update. My favorite! I went to see it, and the entry had a two-story ceiling height and a beautiful spiral staircase where I replaced the ironwork in all the old Hollywood styles of the 40s and 50s. You could just picture the man of the house strolling down the staircase in his velvet smoking jacket with a cigar in one hand and a martini in the other. I painted the entry Tiffany Blue, which made the black and white marble floors I installed pop. This home was purchased by a famous Bollywood movie producer with his exquisite supermodel, Indian wife. Recently, my friend Christine invited me to a Valentino fundraiser in Beverly Hills. I saw the invitation and was so excited, not only because I would see Christine but also because the home I had renovated was hosting the luncheon! I was thrilled to see the owner and how they decorated. Nothing had changed! How serendipitous to know a family loved my style enough not to change anything but some of the decor. They have lived there for 15 years.

While the two houses on Tower Road (which we called "The Twin Towers") were under construction, we purchased a wonderful junior penthouse on the 31st floor right under the two penthouses at Sierra Towers. This building was known for so many famous people living there. It wasn't out of the ordinary to see Elton John or Cher. I never wanted to leave that beautiful condo I had renovated. It was easy living, and every time I walked through the doors, I felt like Peter Pan flying over the city with the view we had. But Michael wanted a "family home" so the boys could come over for our usual family movie and steak nights.

At the same time, I was renovating the condo at Sierra Towers. Michael and I had gone to Carmel for the annual Concours d'Elegance in October. Michael was always buying and selling cars like I did real estate. Cars were his passion. We were driving down Highway 1 along the coast and stopped in the beautiful town of Montecito. To me, there is not a more beautiful place in the world. Since we were living in a condo, we thought it would be fun to find a small place up there and just sell the two tower houses and keep the condo in LA. Building them was fun, but the boys were grown and out of the house. The idea of living in a condo in the city and having a wonderful place to go to on the weekends in Montecito seemed enchanting to me. Thanks to our realtor, Pippa, she found us something out of a storybook. It was an old carriage house with a guest house and garages. There were three enormous arched iron windows and doors that were 15 feet high. That's where the horses and carriages were kept. The huge living room had these wonderful carved beams, and I always thought how funny it was that the horses had no idea how beautiful their environment was. George Washington Smith was the famous architect for many of the world-renowned mansions in that area. I was just happy to have a few acres and the horse carriages. Although beautiful, that house ended up being a heartbreak to me. That's where I discovered, 19 years after the original "discovery," that Michael had been in an affair for two years. It went from being this storybook weekend getaway where our sons and all their friends would come up to being the loneliest place in the world. I can honestly say if I didn't have the Lord, my family, and Jewels, who worked for me but became like a daughter, I wouldn't have made it through. In 25 years of marriage, I designed and renovated 27 homes. Today, I have renovated and restored a total of 42 properties. I always tell people I'm not talented. The Lord just puts the designs in my head, and I have learned 42 times what not to do.

There truly is a reason for my madness. The projects fulfill my creative needs. But most importantly, with every project, I give a large portion of the profits to help ministries and charities. That's really what is important to me. I watched my parents do this all their lives and saw it work. I watched thousands of people's lives touched financially, physically, emotionally, and, most importantly, spiritually. I want to carry on their torch of giving. Through my love for Jesus and through the creativity the Lord has given me, I pray it is just the beginning for me. I am like a kindergarten student jumping up and down, raising my hand and saying, "Pick me, God. Pick me!"

Let's pray together

Jesus, pick me! I will go, and I believe Your Word that says, "We are blessed to be a blessing." Thank you for the ability You have given me to create, as everything good comes from You. Continue to bless my businesses so I can go feed Your sheep. Jesus, You are my CEO! Amen

Chapter 9

God Can Do It Again

I experienced first-hand so much of God's goodness in being faithful when I went through that period of "Why did You let this happen, God?"

It started when I was young. By now, you know that I grew up in a family that took the Bible literally. If Jesus said it, it was the truth to us. That included when He commissioned us to pray for and claim the same miracles He did. He told His disciples to "go out and preach the gospel, lay hands on the sick, and they shall recover." (Mark 16:15-18) As my parents pursued God and grew in the Lord, they asked Jesus for the gift of faith–and He gave it to them. I watched their faith in action and have seen countless people's lives changed.

When my sisters and I were still very young, my mother was diagnosed with an incurable kidney disease called polycystic kidney disease. The kidneys develop cysts that grow until they completely choke the function of the kidney. When that happens, you either have to go on dialysis for the rest of your life or have a kidney transplant. My family believed Jesus was going to heal my mom. But by the time my mom was in her late 60s, her kidneys were functioning at only 10 percent. We never lost faith, but we did realize that God may have another plan, modern medicine. God-given doctor's intelligence can also be miraculous. My mom was too old to go on a donor list. My sisters and I went to UCLA in Los Angeles to one of the best kidney specialists in the world. How grateful we were to have that opportunity. Of the three of us, my older sister, Lisa, was almost a perfect match and accepted as the best option.

Then came the news. After we went through all the testing, I was diagnosed with the same kidney disease as my mother. Through an ultrasound, they detected that my kidneys were covered in cysts. I had had several kidney infections in the past, but it was never diagnosed as polycystic kidney disease. I was merely put on antibiotics.

When my nephrologist sat me down to tell me my diagnosis, this supernatural level of faith that Jesus was going to heal me came over me. I can't explain it. I just knew it. My response to his diagnosis was, "Dr. D, do you believe in God?"

"No. I grew up in Eastern Europe, and I have seen too much war and human suffering to believe there could be a God." To that, I responded, "Perfect."

He looked at me like I had three eyes and asked, "Why is that perfect?" I replied, "Because I have seen healings my entire life. Even Jesus suffered on this Earth. Why should we expect anything different? We live in a fallen world. Suffering is not of God. God is good."

By then, I'm sure he thought I looked like I had not three but four eyes. I continued, "When we experience suffering, God wants to be there to help us and restore us *if*—and that is a very big if—we are willing to believe in Him and turn to Him for help. I believe Jesus is going to heal me. Then, you are going to have to believe in Him. You have already told me there is no cure for this disease. When I'm healed, you will see that God exists."

Dr. D is a world-renowned doctor in his field. He travels all over the world lecturing and teaching about organ diseases. He didn't know how to respond. He just continued with the medical part. Eating healthy could slow this down by about 10 percent, but he emphasized again that there is no cure. I was instructed to come back every three to five years to be monitored or until I started having complications. As I walked down the hallway to leave, Dr. D came to the doorway and called me, "Mrs. Hammer, if you are right, you might just change my life."

I turned around and responded, "No, Dr. D, if I'm right, Jesus is going to change your life."

I walked out, knowing God had a plan. Then for a moment, I walked to my car, I let humanism creep through and thought, "Oh nooooo! What if I am mistaken and I'm not going to be healed? Then I have totally blown it, and Dr. D can say, "I told you there is no God." I said, "God,

You need to show up for me big time!" (Amazing how I keep telling God what He needs to do!)

Then, I collected my thoughts. Wait a minute. I either believe Jesus can heal, or I don't, and I have seen countless miracles in my life. Why is it the hardest to believe in my own healing? I had to go home and stand on all the promises in the Bible about Jesus. It's so easy to let doubt creep into our minds, but God tells us to "meditate on the Word day and night." When I did that, fear and doubt slowly dissipated. Then, when doubt would rear its ugly head again, I would return to the Word and faith was once again restored. Our carnal mind and our faith are constantly in a battle. We have to fight to get it in line with the promises of God. He is either faithful or He is not. I choose to believe He is.

I kept believing that Jesus was going to heal me. Four years after I was diagnosed, a friend stayed in our guest house while he was on a ministry trip in Los Angeles. Louis, an evangelist from Mexico, is an amazing man of God and a prophet. He said he would love to pray for us before he left to catch his flight. Who turns that down? When he got to me, he laid his hands on me and prayed for Jesus to bless me. He had no idea I had been diagnosed with any disease. I hadn't told anyone but family because I believe there is power in our words, and I was not going to claim that diagnosis or even talk about it, giving it any credence.

After he prayed for me, he said, "Dru, this may not make any sense to you, but when I laid my hands on you to pray, I saw these organs. They had big spots and growths all over them. They looked like leopard skin. As I prayed, the spots started falling off one by one."

I started rejoicing. It made all the sense in the world to me. I knew I was healed.

I called Dr. D's office. I told the receptionist I needed to come in for another MRI as soon as possible. I was told my insurance didn't cover another one for another year, but I insisted.

"Why in the world do you want to do this now? Are you having kidney problems?" the receptionist asked. I told her it was just the opposite. I explained that Jesus had healed me and I needed to let Dr. D know.

There was a long pause. Then, politely, "I don't think that is necessary, but I will speak with Dr. D and see if he can order an ultrasound." After begging, pleading, and groveling, she finally just obliged. I went in for the ultrasound, and, of course, they couldn't find any spots. I was whooping and hollering like I was at the Super Bowl. In walked Dr. D, not humored at all. He managed to say something like, "Well, you know, Dru, this is a different test, and the MRI shows much more. The cysts just may not show up on this ultrasound."

I said, "I was diagnosed from an ultrasound. They could see the spots clearly. Then you ordered an MRI for further confirmation." I figured this would be a little (or a lot) less perplexing to a self-proclaimed atheist.

That day, I bought Dr. D a Bible with his name embossed on it. That way, he couldn't recycle it and might feel guilty for throwing something away with his name on it. I also brought him books by genius men just like him, such as C.S. Lewis 'Mere Christianity. Mr. Lewis was an atheist but came to know God on a deep, personal level when he researched the Old Testament/Torah and New Testament and saw how Jesus filled over 324 biblical prophecies of the coming Messiah. I told Dr. D, "I know you are a well-educated man with years and years of research and studies, so here is something new to study. If this is all true, then I'm talking about eternity. What have you really got to lose? If I'm wrong, your outcome won't be any different than what you believe now. How do you pass up something as important as this?"

He had no words. I hugged him, leaving a "goodie bag" of a Bible and books that I'm sure he dreaded receiving. I walked out, knowing the Lord had me there to speak truth into his life, plant those seeds, and use this gift of healing for His glory.

After I moved from Los Angeles, I continued my annual checkups wherever I was living. I'm delighted to say my kidneys are functioning perfectly. I've even seen new doctors over the years and told them I had polycystic kidneys, and they all tell me that's impossible because your kidney numbers are perfect.

The God of impossibilities.

My mom, on the other hand, got her healing through medical expertise, and my sister Lisa donated her kidney. My family was so faithful in praying and believing God would heal her; we knew it would happen one way or another.

Only God knows why I was healed miraculously and why my mom and sister had to go through surgery. We do know He had a plan right there in the Baylor Hospital in Dallas where they had the surgery. My dad had never been one to sit around. While my mom and sister were in the hospital, he couldn't sit still. He walked the hallways and spoke about Jesus with every patient, their families, nurses, doctors, and the cleaning crew. We were a little mortified when he would just walk into hospital rooms unannounced, making sure everyone knew Jesus. Yet they all seemed touched by his prayers and did not seem to mind. People are desperate for hope, especially in a hospital.

My dad walked into a room of an older couple. The man was a garbage collector by trade, and his wife had the same kidney disease as my mom. He was retired but had to go back to work to be able to pay for all the deductibles on the kidney transplant surgery. The loyal husband would leave in the middle of the night to get to his job, which was two hours away. Then, he would drive back late that evening to be next to his wife in the hospital.

My dad asked if they would like him to pray for them. You know, the "usual" in our family. That day was the seventh day of the woman being in the hospital. The doctors said if the kidney did not "take" in seven days, then the body would not accept the foreign kidney. They would have to send her home because there was nothing more they could do. That day, her kidney function was flatlined on the monitor. They were devastated after all the sacrifices they had made. Desperate, they welcomed my dad to come in and pray for them. They had loved the Lord all their life. My dad's faith reached up to God on their behalf. He asked Jesus to come touch this woman to heal her new kidney and make it function perfectly. As soon as they were finished praying, the monitors started going up and down. Her new kidney began functioning! They went home restored, physically and spiritually. If my mom and Lisa had to have surgery just so we were in that place at that time for that couple, it was worth it. I sometimes wonder how many other people's lives have been touched, healed, and restored by their story.

We all had dinner together several nights we were there and rejoiced at all the miraculous stories our dad would tell us. Was it our choice for my mom and sister to have to go through a major surgery like that? Of course not. But God knew my dad. He put him to work, and in the meantime, our prayers were answered for my mom's healing. The surgeons told us that at her age, she would be "lucky" to get 10 years out of that kidney. Well, we don't believe in luck, and it's a good thing. Over 21 years later, mom's kidney functioned perfectly in her body when the Lord called her home.

About six years ago, I saw Dr. Byrd, an amazing Godly doctor in Palm Desert, for my annual checkup. I shared with him how I was diagnosed with polycystic kidneys 10 years earlier. Then I told him how Jesus healed me from that disease. Dr. Byrd not only believed me, but he said he had seen many miracles in his medical practice. He did all my blood work and asked me to come back in a few days when he had the results. Not surprisingly, my kidneys are functioning without fail. Dr. Byrd said if I still had polycystic kidneys, there would be no way that my numbers would be absolutely perfect. We had church right there in his office and ended up talking for over an hour about the faithfulness of God.

This miracle—amongst many in my life—didn't just happen for my benefit. I believe Jesus heals us to give others hope and spread His good news. I have the privilege of sharing the faithfulness of God with others, which is truly the joy of my life. That is what I have been called to do.

Let's pray together

Jesus, Your words are By My stripes you were healed," and I take You at Your Word. Thank you for dying on the cross for our healing and eternal life with You in heaven. You may not always heal in the way we want You to, but You always heal, and the ultimate healing is when we get to be face-to-face with our Savior in heaven. I am going to take my healing and share it with the world. I love You because You loved me first. Amen

Chapter 10

Showing Up

In God's kingdom, things seem diametrically opposite to how they work in this world. It seems totally unnatural to give when you are in need, but that's exactly what the Bible tells us to do. In times of need, you give.

"Give and it will be given to you. A good measure, pressed down, shaken together, and running over will be put into your bosom. For with the same measure that you use, it will be measured back to you." (Luke 6:38, NKJV) This applies to our finances, our health, and our hearts.

Fourteen years before I had any inkling that I would be going through a divorce, I heard about the Los Angeles Dream Center from our friend, Justin. When I toured the ministry center, I was astounded by how they were helping people from all kinds of addictions, turmoil, brokenness, etc. I was also absolutely amazed at how many people were giving up everything to move there to help other hurting people.

A young man named Matthew Barnett started the Dream Center when he moved to Los Angeles to take over Angelus Temple, a struggling church in Echo Park, a rough area of town. Aimee Semple McPherson built the church when the "world of ministers" came against her. She began her ministry in the early 1920s when women were not allowed to preach in the pulpit. That wasn't going to stop her. She started her own denomination, Foursquare, and built her own church in the heart of Los Angeles. What I love the most is Aimee's faith. She hired an architect and builders to build the Angeles Temple, and her architect came to her and said, "Aimee, we only have enough money to dig the hole for the foundation." She looked at him and said, "Then dig the hole." Oh, to have that kind of faith, and that is exactly why the Lord chose her. At that time, over 10 percent of the population of Los Angeles had attended her church. Not many churches, especially in huge cities, can claim that today. She saved hundreds of thousands of people from starvation during the Depression. She sold more war bonds than anyone in the country and held healing services where people would come and wait in long lines for hours outside her church building for Jesus to heal them. If that wasn't enough, she started her own radio station and preached the gospel to millions. Over eight million people worldwide today are still Foursquare denominational members. How many male pastors can say that? Just a thought. It seems to me God had a plan bigger than man's limitations.

Eighty years later, the large Angelus Temple church Aimee built had come into disrepair. Echo Park had become gang-infested with a very high crime rate. When the church was looking for a new pastor, potential families would fly in, see the area, and promptly leave on the next plane. They couldn't imagine raising their children in that dangerous area of Los Angeles. Not so for the young Matthew Barnett—a whopping 20 years of age. Where others saw disaster, he saw opportunity. When he came to the congregation, it dwindled to about 15 people. A gang member was shot and killed right on the front step the first Sunday Matthew showed up to preach. Not exactly a recipe for success in a church, but Matthew, the strong-willed wrestling champion, would not be deterred. He visited the family of the gang member who had died, took them bags of groceries, and invited them to his church. To this day, the family attends that church. Radical changes have happened to not only that family but thousands of former gang members and their families.

On the day of the shooting, Matthew moved his desk out on the front church steps as if to say, "I'm not leaving."

Today, the Dream Center offers over 700 free beds to those in need, serves around 1,000 hot meals every day, and provides groceries to around 35,000 people every month. Crime in the neighborhood has also substantially decreased since they opened the doors to the community.

Matthew, his beautiful wife, Caroline, who started the food ministry, and his father, pastor Tommy Barnett, made such a lowball offer they had no idea they would even be close to getting the asbestos-riddled building that motorcycle gangs and rats called home. When the nuns, who wanted the Lord's ministry to continue, accepted the offer, they didn't even have the money for the down payment. They began to pray. Not only didn't they have the money to buy the building, but each floor also took over a million dollars in repair to get up to code and livable. They purchased the old City of Angels Hospital with over 400,000 square feet. Today, the Dream Center has 14 finished floors, each floor housing different perils of men and women who come in to be, as they say, "not rehabilitated but restored to Christ."

Only a few floors had been finished when my family was first introduced to the Dream Center. We got to participate and watch how God sent people in "for such a time as this" to help finish the building. The project was like the "loaves and fishes" in the Book of Mark— money was multiplying and coming in from miraculous places. When Michael and I went to the board meetings, anyone in their right mind would've called the project virtually impossible. That's when God does His greatest work–when it looks the most impossible in man's eyes. God wants us to look to Him. Miracles happen when people diligently pray and roll their sleeves up to do their part. I believe God is still in the miracle business.

I always say, "The gospel is free, but ministry is expensive." When people enter the discipleship program, they often come off the streets with nothing but clothes on their backs and in desperate need. The one-year (sometimes it takes two or three years) program is free of charge to those in need. God calls us to tithe and give offerings so ministries like this can exist. I wanted to do more than just write checks. I wanted to give my time and love people who are so broken.

I called the church to see how I could get more involved. I loved their response. "We want you to pray about how you can help. When you begin, the women you will work with will immediately be attached to you. They have had enough betrayal and disappointment in their lives. So, you need to be consistent, and if you can commit, you need to keep showing up."

Michael and I had a crazy travel schedule and many other commitments, most importantly, being there for our young teenage boys. But I knew I just had to make time for this. The first thing I decided to do was throw a big birthday party once a month for the women who had birthdays in that month. I had 20 pizzas delivered, a big birthday cake, and gift bags with luxury items and squishy blankets for all the birthday girls. The first time I threw the party, a woman in her 40s came up to me with tears in her eyes and said, "This is the first birthday party anyone has ever had for me." I simply couldn't imagine. That broke me and made me realize even more how blessed my life has been.

I had no idea what I was doing. I had never dealt with women who came out of heroin addiction, alcoholism, prostitution, or any kind of abuse. I had a political science degree, for crying out loud (and still can't figure out how the Electoral College works). But that is one of the amazing things I love about God. He isn't looking for ability. He is looking for availability. I would spend hours with the women, listening to them when they needed to share and just loving on them. When I first started, I would often get in my car and cry all the way home. I couldn't leave behind the tragic stories. I'd say to the Lord, "God, what in the world have I gotten myself into? I don't know what to say to them or how to relate to them." And Jesus, in that sweet, gentle voice, that 'knowing' voice, said to me, "Dru, all you have to do is pray, show up, and love them. I will do the rest." Well, thankfully, I can do all three of those. For 10 years, I just kept showing up.

After I had worked with them for a while, I decided to step it up a bit. I began taking them to a Mexican restaurant. They loved it because it was an all-you-could-eat buffet. We were the only group of women they probably lost money on. It was a great change from the institutional food they were being served. However, they were grateful for that food, too, since many came in from malnutrition. I would take that opportunity at the luncheons to share the love of Christ with them and confirm all they are being taught in the program. I would have one-on-one time with each of them. After a few years, we moved our lunches to the Cheesecake Factory. They loved going to a restaurant where the cheesecake slices seemed to be bigger than their problems. We began having outings every week I was in town. Then I started taking them to movies if I could find one that didn't have any violence and/or sex scenes. They had already experienced enough of that. I had to sit through a lot of animated features, much like when my boys were young. Justin Bieber's movie was the women's favorite. Perhaps his story of having a single mother, Pattie, with no means and barely making it through life, even pressured to have an abortion, which she refused, spoke to these beautiful women. So many of them were abandoned by their fathers or, worse, beaten and sexually abused by them. This story of redemption gave them hope. They began to believe God also had a plan for their lives.

I remember a fun Christmas party that ended at Sephora. Each woman got a gift card to go wild and buy makeup. You would have thought they had gotten a million dollars. They spent hours picking out what they wanted. In the meantime, Sephora treated them to makeovers and manicures. I will always be grateful to Sephora for helping the women feel so special. One woman, who had been homeless and had been addicted to heroin for 20 years, looked in the mirror after her makeover and started to cry. She said, "I'm beautiful." There wasn't a dry eye in the place.

I cannot describe the joy they brought into my life. As my son used to joke, "Mom, you went all over Los Angeles ministering to women, and you finally found a group of women who would listen to you." Little did I know how these women would turn the tables and pour love into my life when I needed it the most.

The Dream Center staff eventually asked me if I would consider working with human trafficked victims. Of course, I was happy to do anything they asked me to do. I was a work in progress on how to speak and minister to these women. I had learned a lot. However, this was a whole other depth of despair I wasn't sure I was ready to handle. But sometimes, God throws us into the deep end. I would have chickened out if I had "waded" from the shallow end toward the deep end.

I had absolutely no idea what I was going to do or say when speaking with women who escaped human trafficking. With over 100 women in each program, there was no way I could spend quality time with all of them at each event. I had my dear friends Nina, Tina, Kelly, Carolyn, Gerri, and Julie, who were also faithful in working the room, providing a listening ear and loving arms for these women.

Nina, who never missed an event at the Dream Center, came with me that very first day of my new 'assignment. 'I could not have done it without her. We prayed as we drove to meet them, asking God to give us wisdom. We knew nothing about what really goes on in human trafficking, but we were about to learn quickly. We sat outside at a favorite restaurant on a beautiful Los Angeles day. Six women joined us. We began making small talk. We didn't ask them any questions. When they trusted us and were ready to talk, they would. Finally, they started sharing their stories when they became comfortable and knew we were there to help them. Nina and I were so horrified by what they told us. We both had to fight back tears. To say that they were treated like animals would be incorrect. Animals wouldn't treat each other that way. One woman told us how her "pimp daddy" was a Vietnam War vet. He used the same tactics on her that were used on him when he was tortured in Vietnam. She was caged with strobe lights so she couldn't sleep. She was beaten with baseball bats in the cage to psychologically beat her down so she would be submissive and not ever run away. As we sat there, I started getting sick to my stomach. After she finished telling her story, I naively remarked, "Why would you call him pimp daddy? A daddy is someone who loves you and wants to take care of you."

1,000 people came to our wedding in Tulsa, OK at the beautiful First United Methodist church. It was January and 19 degrees—Uncle Viktor flew straight in from Palm Beach wearing his seersucker suit.

The original brothers, Armand and Victor in 1985. Victor found Jesus through my dad just four months before he had a stroke and died.

The four generations: Armand, Julian, Michael and little Armie having one of our family Sunday suppers together in 1988, right before Viktor was born.

Armand "Armie" and Viktor "Happy" with their lab, Tara in Dallas, TX in 1993. They've never forgiven me for the years of bowl cuts :)

Dr. Armand Hammer visited the hospital when our second son was born asking us to name him Viktor after his brother. We obliged.

Armie and Viktor when we first moved to the Cayman Islands in 1994.

One of our Sunday suppers, after getting home from church. This was taken just six months before Armand "Boompa" accepted Jesus as his Messiah. He passed away in 1990, one year after this photo was taken.

Family ski trip in Deer Valley, UT in 1995. The boys surpassed us the first time we took them skiing when they were just 3 and 5 years old.

Flying out to a western affair in 2006 with our cowboy boots. When in Texas...

London with Dr. Armand Hammer and his wife Frances in 1987. First time Michael and I met Prince Charles and Princess Diana.

Black tie affair with Michael in 2005.

My parents, Douglas and Donna Mobley, at Armie's wedding in 2010, right before my marriage crashed.

On the set of *The Lone Ranger* in Sante Fe, NM with Armie in 2012. My hair turned white from the stress of the divorce.

Together with my son, Viktor, at a luncheon for Childhelp in Newport Beach, CA in 2015.

Second trip to Israel in 2022, after walking through the tunnels of Hezekiah with Kathie Lee Gifford and Lesley Burbridge. This time, restored and wearing Hammered Heart t-shirts.

Trying to put on a happy face at my dad's burial in 2023. Every year we gave dad a new pair of New Balance running shoes, so we wore them in honor of him.

My two favorite people in the world at an event together at the Hammer Museum in Los Angeles, CA.

My dad and sisters, Lisa and Mel "Honeybee", at our mother's funeral. My dad lost his soulmate of almost 65 years. The moment mom went to Heaven, my dad worshiped and thanked the Lord for the years he had with his bride.

While visiting my grandchildren, Harper and Ford, in the Cayman Islands, Elizabeth took my favorite photo ever.

A photo taken of Viktor by his wife, Angie, who is a wonderful photographer

Renovation of Henry Mancini's home. Just two examples inside and out of the 27 homes I renovated while living in Los Angeles, CA.

Inside of Mancini's country French home we purchased in Holmby Hills—all of his original sheet music was wallpapered in his office, like *The Pink Panther* music.

The living room of our Tower Road home in Beverly Hills. This is the home I ended up living alone in during our divorce.

Outside of the same Tower Road home. Amazing how a happy family home just becomes a house—I liken it to a body without a soul.

Uh oh! It was like I hit the eject button, and her wheels came off with every expletive you could imagine.

She ended with, "Don't ever talk smack about my pimp daddy!"

At that point, I was out to sea without a life raft. I responded, "I'm sorry if I hurt you. I would never intentionally hurt you. I love you." Then, more expletives, "You don't @&#ing love me."

I just looked at her and said, "Well, I'm just going to have to prove to you that I love you and keep showing up." And that's exactly what I did. I just kept showing up. I learned that day that there is a strange "soul tie" that a prostitute has with her pimp, and you never say a word against them until the Lord breaks that soul tie.

Nina and I got into my car to drive home. For the first 10 minutes we couldn't even speak. Then Nina said, "What in the world was that?" We both burst into tears and cried the rest of the way home. It would take us a long time to truly realize the depth of despair these women had to live in—how the devil (through men) had ravaged their lives.

To my utter amazement, when I crashed and burned with my unexpected divorce, those women were a big part of my healing. They showed up. I know their "cuts" were much deeper than mine, but in the moment I was faced with the fact that I had been sexually and financially betrayed, they were there. As horrible as it was for me, I couldn't even imagine what my Dream Center ladies had gone through most of their lives. Only God knows the future, and I marvel at how He prepared me with so many years of teaching women the importance of forgiveness even when the perpetrators don't deserve forgiveness. Jesus didn't tell us to forgive only the small things but to forgive all. Now, I was faced with the challenge of forgiveness. I would always tell them it doesn't hurt the perpetrator if you don't forgive. I was convinced they had moved on to abusing other women, but it hurts the abused if we are not able to let the hurt go.

When I returned home, I was utterly devastated by what I heard and for allowing myself to become the victim. Wow, now I can look back and see the hand of God throwing me into the deep end with ladies who have been through so much worse. Many mornings, I didn't think I could get out of bed. I had to practice all I had been teaching at the Dream Center. These beautiful women were my inspiration, and they taught me that I had to get up, keep going, and forgive.

Amid my devastation, God gave me a much-needed miracle. I called to book the reservation for our monthly lunch with the entire group from the Dream Center. We usually ran up a sizable bill as the program began growing. There could be almost a hundred women at a time, so the restaurant always wanted a deposit when I booked the reservation. The restaurant called me back; my credit card was declined. I couldn't believe it. It had to be a mistake. I called our office to double-check. Nope, not a mistake. All my credit cards, including the charitable account, had been canceled. I was so upset I couldn't even see straight. In the 25 years that we were married, our money went into joint accounts. I assumed, maybe foolishly, that what is mine was his and what is his was mine. Even though I brought in more income on the houses I worked on than Michael had made in his work, his office had control over everything. Without warning, the office cut off all my credit cards, closed all the bank accounts, and moved them into separate accounts. It's a lesson to all women and me: never let anyone have full control over your money, and be aware of everything you sign. Who would ever imagine this would even be an issue? Well, now I do, and this can happen to anyone.

At that moment, I didn't have any funds to pay for this ministry I was involved with for years. This was much more than just my accounts being closed. These women counted down the days to having an afternoon out and taking a break from the very difficult routine of healing. I called the office thinking, naively, that there must be a mistake. I started bawling after I hung up the phone. My husband's office had total control over me and, even worse, my Dream Center girls. The betrayal was shocking and devastating at the same time.

My carnal mind kicked in with the "How dare he?" and "Who does he think he is?"

That would be the G-rated version. Even if I hadn't contributed to our finances, I couldn't believe a man who supposedly loved me could treat me this way. I kept thinking in my mind how these luncheons were not for me. They were for the women I was helping.

Here I was alone in my big house, feeling so rejected and discarded, like I was a piece of chattel. Michael had no concern for my well-being. I stewed all night, having make-believe conversations with Michael for hours, ripping him up and down. Unfortunately, this was just the beginning of what I had to endure from a man who was punishing me because I refused to "look the other way." I cried and prayed but didn't tell a soul at first what had happened. I mean, not only was it cruel, but it was also embarrassing. After all, our friends had seen us in supposedly such a loving relationship for 25 years. Was it all fake? Did he ever love me?

That next day, my friend Tina called. She wanted to take me to lunch to meet the person who is head of public relations at her family's shopping center, The Grove in Los Angeles. I hadn't slept a wink the night before, but Tina was such a good friend, and I said I would love to join her. As we sat down to lunch, they asked me about my work with the women at the Dream Center. After I told them, they looked at each other and said, "Yes, this would be a perfect fit. We would like to host you and take care of this when you come to dinner at the Cheesecake Factory." They also said they would host the movies in their shopping center. Talk about God's perfect timing. This was the day after all my accounts were closed. There's simply no way Tina would have known that.

I was once again reminded that when you keep showing up, God shows up. He provides, and He does it sooooo much better. From then on, not only were we hosted, but a table was always waiting for us instead of needing to get there an hour early to put our names in at the restaurant. When we went to the movies, they reserved our seats with a security guard, making sure no one took them. They even had water bottles and popcorn on each chair. Years later, I found out that my friend Tina had personally hosted all those events. She didn't want me to know. Could there be a better friend? My cup runneth over. That was nothing short of a miracle. God uses people as His hands for His miracles. Thank you, Tina, for being His hands.

Every time I showed up at the Dream Center, I heard atrocities of things that were done to these amazing, strong women. It was always so humbling. One woman told me her story about how she tried to escape from her abusive boyfriend. She had run away from home because of an abusive father. Since she had nowhere to go, she started stripping at this man's strip club, thinking she had no other option. Soon, the owner of the strip club began abusing her. After the abuse became unbearable, she tried to escape. As she was running away in the middle of the night, he got in his truck, ran her over, and tried to kill her. She ended up in the hospital. For three months, she was in a coma until she finally woke up. She had a huge scar on her forehead of a swastika put there by her "boyfriend" with a knife. He wanted to leave his "mark" so she would never forget whom she belonged to. I was praying with her and counseling her on the importance of forgiveness so she could have freedom in her future. That is God's truth, but easier said than done. This kind of situation is bigger than we are, and that is exactly why we need a loving God to help us when we are incapable.

The Bible states to not only forgive "seven times, but seventy times seven." For her to forgive her perpetrator, she had to look in the mirror every day and be reminded of what that man had done to her. It's so easy to counsel on forgiveness when you haven't been in the other individual's shoes. When I was betrayed, I had to step up to bat myself and "put my money where my mouth was." During my divorce, I knew I had to keep showing up. I couldn't disappoint my women. And every time I showed up, they would run up to me and ask, "How did your court date go? Are you okay? We have been praying for you." I could never leave there having a pity party. After all those years of showing up, little did I know I would get much more out of serving them than they ever got from me. "Give, and it shall be given unto you."

Divorce is never God's plan "A" but when things happen beyond our control, he always has another plan for us. Divorce is never the ending of our story, it can be the beginning of a new beautiful one, IF we are able to shake it off and forgive. That one gets a "hallelujah."

Let's pray together

Thank you, Jesus, for the gift of forgiveness. Only with You could I truly forgive my husband, Michael. Even though I didn't think he deserved it. I love you for always showing me grace and mercy and helping me show that toward others. Amen

Chapter 11

Loss & Love

I had to walk the talk of what I had been teaching the beautiful women at the Dream Center for years. I had watched my parents walk out their faith, even when it was hard. I learned so much from them. So, you can imagine that one of the things I dreaded the most was telling my parents about the divorce. After all, they had been praying for the right husband for my sisters and me since we were children. They always told us that apart from deciding to serve the Lord, choosing a mate was the most important decision we would ever make. They were right; all three of us chose men who loved the Lord and seemed to be the perfect fit for us.

Michael was a new believer when we married, unlike myself, who was exposed to the Lord my entire life. I could have never married someone who didn't believe and didn't have a relationship with Christ, as He is my number one priority. I needed someone whose priority was in alignment with mine. The problem was I had the advantage of growing up in the ways of the Lord since I was five years old. Michael was brand new to these beliefs, and the learning curve was steep. Therefore, I was always the spiritual leader in the family, which really wasn't my rightful place (Ephesians 5:22). In all fairness, he had no idea what he was getting into. I had him praying in tongues within a few months of meeting him. Next thing he knew, we were reading the Bible every day together, going to church twice a week, and driving the boys to Malibu every Friday night for a youth group.

Looking back, it might have been a little overwhelming. Probably more than a little. I'm sure Michael felt like he had landed in the center of a tornado (as a friend of mine calls me "Drunado"). But in his defense, he appeared to take it all amazingly well and seemed to really want that life. I have been called many things, but I don't think subservient is one of them. I know what I want in life. Some may call it bossy, but it may just be downright driven. But Michael had come from an abusive father and a scattered family life. He seemed to love the entire package I was able to offer him of a devoted wife, two amazing sons, and a wonderful family who loved him as much as I did.

I was a loyal, good wife. I'm not saying that to be boastful. I had amazing role models, and I knew what to do and would never be anything but loyal. I was what many would call old-fashioned and did everything for him. I waited on him hand and foot. Yet, looking back, he was actually so compliant when I threw him into the "radical Christian world deep end." I was also a bit much in my style. I cleaned out everything I felt was ugly that he owned, right down to his '70s macrame pot hangers. I probably didn't give him much choice. But I assumed Michael was looking for a change in his life when he met me. He knew the life he once lived would be the end of him. He told me how several times he was on cocaine binges, and many times he felt his heart was going to burst, thinking he was dying. People want peace, love, and joy in their lives. I think he felt I could offer that. It was a small price to pay to ditch the '70s hippie-style decor.

What you can call me is resilient. I don't give up very easily. So, when my marriage crashed and burned, I still had this thought in my head that it was all going to be okay. About six weeks into the crash and burn, I was in Aspen when Michael called me, upset. Would I please come back to Los Angeles? My birthday was in a few days. He bought something for me and wanted to take me to dinner and talk about everything.

Any woman knows—to be wooed back, to hear that he loves you and wants to do anything in the world to get you back—that's all you want. After all, it's what happens in the movies. And any man knows that buying a woman a gift (and boy, did he buy great gifts) is the dangling carrot that gets your attention, but love and affection "closes the deal." That's in the movies, too.

Skeptical and hopeful, I agreed to fly back and have dinner with him. We went out for a beautiful steak dinner. He brought me a large, gift-wrapped box and placed it on the table. We ordered a bottle of wine. Once again, I took very few sips. We discussed things, trying to be calm and friendly, which was difficult for me knowing about all the betrayals. As we finished dinner, I asked, "I just have one question for you. Why were you so willing to take the chance of losing your family for moments of pleasure when we have such a loving history together and what I thought was a wonderful life and family together?" He held his glass of wine, shrugged his shoulders and said, "Because it was fun."

How in the world do you respond to that? I don't know if I was crushed or just hacked off that he could be so insensitive. It was very apparent that there was zero remorse, let alone repentance. I was so sucker punched by his words. It would have hurt less if he had just punched me in the face. He just didn't care. Plus, I hired a private investigator, and he was still seeing and speaking to the mistress daily. I had to get out. It has been said that "Men are from Mars and Women are from Venus." That's certainly true emotionally. When I told my girlfriends, they were appalled. When I told my male friends, they said, "Well, at least he was honest." See, different planets.

If sin weren't fun, no one would do it. I'm sure he had a ball (pardon the pun) doing whatever he wanted. I loved him and couldn't imagine being with anyone else. But I knew it was over when I saw how he could be so cavalier and smug about it. You can't work things out with an unrepentant man.

Looking back, maybe I shouldn't have been so blindsided. Michael first had an affair seven years into our marriage. One day I unexpectedly went up to the office to visit him. I was in the area, and it was the children's naptime, so I thought I would see if Michael wanted to have lunch. I walked in, and I could cut the atmosphere with a knife. I was in typical mom casual wear, and the secretary was in a tight sweater, pencil skirt, and six-inch spiked heels. I know, very cliche. I later learned Michael had paid for her new, enormous breasts. I knew the minute I walked in by both of their awkwardness that I was interrupting "their space." When you know, you know. I found out I am much tougher than I thought. After a week of very, shall I say, uncomfortable conversations and Michael rarely coming home, I packed up the boys and Luz, and we flew to Tulsa to be with my parents. Thankfully, it was during the summer. I told my parents that we needed a break from all the construction and that we would stay for a month or so. Of course, they were thrilled. I had to pretend to be excited. I was stoic and didn't shed a tear. I dug my heels in and wasn't planning on going back. But then I would watch my two precious boys and how excited they got when they would talk with their daddy on the phone. During prayer times, they always prayed for their daddy and asked when he was coming. Michael eventually flew in, even though I didn't want him to. He was repentant. I either had to believe God's word on the importance of forgiving, or I had to pack up my Christian walk. It came down to this: I loved Michael, and my children needed and wanted their father. I had to walk my talk if Michael was truly repentant and was going to change the errs of his ways. He convinced me his affair was over after I packed up and showed tough love. I guess it wasn't as much fun for him when he had to come home to an empty house. I forgave and believed we had this perfect family again–until we didn't.

What I didn't know was that the affair had continued, and that was not the only one. Maybe Michael was really good at disguising his life. Or maybe I just chose to be dumb and naive. All I knew was my mother could trust my father. Michael was always "lovey-dovey" with me. I think he was able to compartmentalize this need for the affirmation of other women due to his severe abuse as a child. It wasn't like we didn't get along or enjoy each other. We were best friends and in love with each other. He was always home at night. Afternoon delights seemed to be his forte.

Now, all these years later, his attitude was totally different. His arrogance was like a slap in the face. At that moment, I knew it was over for good. I grabbed the beautiful Hermes 'Kelly bag he bought me for my birthday (I earned that dumb bag!) and walked out of the restaurant. I called a cab and moved into the guest room. How silly am I? Why didn't I kick him out of our bed and move him into the guest room? It was all such a blur of brokenness I couldn't make sense of any of it. Where is that handbook—or movie—to tell me what to do?

While none of that was easy, I knew sharing this news with my parents would be the worse. I knew I had to do it before I filed, and they heard it through the grapevine. I called my sisters with the news first. I now laugh at how differently my two sisters handled the call when I told them what Michael had done. Lisa, the tough one, would have driven to our house and literally cut his kahunas off. Don't mess with "Mona" (as she is called). My younger sister Mel was driving in her car and started sobbing so hard she had to pull over. I had to console her, telling her to pull herself together. Wait, shouldn't the roles be reversed?

Then I told my sisters that, in no uncertain terms, they had to be there when I told our parents. "I'm not asking. I'm summoning you. I need you two there. I'm sending you plane tickets to Tulsa, and I'll see you in a few days."

My sisters are the best. We all would drop everything in the world to be there for each other. They held me up through the entire ordeal. When I called our parents and told them the three of us were coming to visit, my mom said, "I am so thrilled you three are coming. What a treat to have just the three of you to ourselves. We are all going to have so much fun."

If only. I had divorce papers delivered the day I got to Tulsa so I could sign them and start the process. Mom and dad picked us up at the airport, and we all went to dinner. I maintained a smile. I didn't want to get into everything until we got home. When we did, I sat down and told them the inevitable. Afterward, I held my breath. I worried I would·get the lecture of needing to stay and let the Lord work it out. Which, of course, I agreed 100 percent that God could heal our marriage. But I also knew that the man, now known as my "hasband," had moved on. It takes two to want to work things out. To my relief, my dad said, "Dru, I already knew. I was playing tennis the other day, and the Lord spoke to me and told me. You have done all you can do, and you must get out. God said to me that you are to be 'as wise as a serpent and harmless as a dove.'"

Knowing he supported my decision, I felt like a thousand pounds had been lifted off my back. My mom couldn't process the whole thing at first. After I explained everything, she asked me, "Is Michael still going to come to the hill country with us for our 55th wedding anniversary over Thanksgiving?" Uh… she was not really processing this info.

Honestly, divorce was such a foreign idea for her, especially in her own family. From that night on, the horrible process of divorce was in the works. I had my attorney file on Halloween. I've never liked Halloween anyway.

I filed at 4:50 p.m. before the courthouse closed at 5:00 p.m. My attorney said it would go under the radar since it was a closing day before a "holiday" (if that's what you call Halloween). I walked out of that divorce with about a fourth of what I had made. I know, dumb, but it happens and trust me, today that wouldn't have happened…lesson learned.

The last day I was in Tulsa, my parents were going to lunch with old friends. I just couldn't get myself to meet them for lunch. I didn't want to pretend everything was wonderful, but I also wasn't ready to get into the mud and talk about all that was happening.

Instead, I hopped in the shower and got ready to catch my flight back to Los Angeles. When I got into the shower, something happened that I hadn't expected. I completely fell apart. I seemed to be so strong and stoic when I was with my family, but suddenly, the floodgates opened. I couldn't hold the strong act together anymore. I began weeping and thinking in my mind, "Oh, God. What have I done? Now that I've told my parents, there is no turning back. Jesus, please give me a sign I did the right thing by telling them." I finally got myself out of the shower and was trying to pull myself together when the phone rang. It was an old friend I hadn't seen in years. She had just run into my parents at lunch and wanted to come over to see me before I left town. My parents didn't tell her what was happening, but they knew my friend had previously gone through a divorce and suggested she call me. "You might be a good person for Dru to talk to if you have time to see her." I wasn't up for company, but I knew it would be good to talk to an old friend. Within a few minutes, she rang the doorbell. She and her new husband had just gotten back to Tulsa the day before from a cruise in Europe. She had not seen my parents in a few years and was happy to run into them. Since I was still so raw from the shower episode, I spilled my guts out to her. Surprisingly, my friend already knew something was wrong. On the last night of their cruise, they were seated next to a couple whose husband worked in the business Armand had started, Occidental Petroleum. When the conversation came to where they were from, my friends mentioned they lived in Tulsa. The couple asked, "Do you know Dru Hammer?" My friend told them she had known me for over 40 years. The man proceeded to tell her that he had known me since

Michael and I first got married. He was worried about me because he knew Michael had been cheating on me for a long time.

As crushing as that was to hear, I was also amazed at the perfect timing of the Lord. For me, answers from the Lord rarely come within 15 minutes of asking, but I needed a miracle at that moment.

The Lord heard me cry out in the shower and sent a friend to tell me what I needed to hear. It was time to pull myself up by my bootstraps. By sending a friend, God allowed me to see more of the truth–that this was a chronic problem in our marriage and something that was known. I may not have wanted to believe it, but it was my reality. No woman (or man) deserves to be in a relationship of betrayal. Eventually, darkness always comes to light. God promises us that, and He is incapable of telling a lie. Unfortunately, the truth hurts sometimes. But sometimes, we just need to know, as information is power. Then, we can move on and be able to do what we have to do. The Lord released me at that moment. That final blow was a deep cut, and I was no longer in denial.

Yes, I made the mistake of hiring a detective to dig for information. That did nothing but put salt in my wounds, so that didn't last long. God has always been faithful in showing me what I needed to know and when I needed to know it. This is where the saying "ignorance is bliss" may come in. Many people asked me, "Was Michael with one woman or were there many?" My answer was always, "What difference does it make? Cheating is cheating, and I would rather not know the details. I know all I need to know."

I got back on the plane to Los Angeles, knowing what I had to do. God doesn't like divorce. It's never His will for our lives and our families. However, when His plans are thwarted due to human failures, He always has a "backup plan" for our lives. Sometimes it's a tortuous journey to get there. As I headed back home, I didn't realize the reality of losing everything dear to me would hit me like a ton of bricks. I lost control during that season and became this emaciated wanderer. It wasn't pretty. And it was only the beginning.

Let's pray together

In the darkest of times, God, I know You are there. When all I could pray was   help," You heard me, comforted me, and moved on my behalf. Amen

Chapter 12

Forrest Gump

The divorce process can pummel any decent human being into an unrecognizable state. That certainly was my case. Not only was I unrecognizable to myself, I was anything but myself to others. One afternoon at my home, it became particularly clear.

We had decided on private mediation with a retired judge. This way, our divorce wouldn't be exposed in court papers and wouldn't be printed in public newspapers. Hammer was a known name in Los Angeles for a company Armand had built, a museum he created for his art collection and all the charity work. Our crumbling marriage fiasco wouldn't have made a front-page story, but it probably would have been in the pages somewhere. We all know happy news doesn't sell newspapers. Good, juicy gossip does. No matter what page it would have landed on, I didn't want my children exposed to this.

Before going into each mediation meeting, I would beg God for help. Then, I would walk in and get pulverized by Michael's team of attorneys. I would hold onto scriptures like "He will fight our battles for us" and "I can do all things through Christ who strengthens me." In hindsight, I realize that as Christians, we will lose some battles, but we will win the war in the end. So, I would put on my armor of God and just keep showing up. Even though I was feeling completely defeated in the process. I couldn't eat, couldn't concentrate, and was an emaciated version of myself. Zsa Zsa Gabor said, "After 50 years old, it's either your face or your ass." Boy, was that true. I was a size zero, but my face looked 20 years older.

I turned to the most loyal friend and person in the world, Sylvia, my former pastor from the Malibu Vineyard. Sylvia had recently lost her husband to cancer, so we both were at a devastating time in our lives. I would come home and call her, and we would talk until the wee hours of the night. We both were grieving at losing our spouses. She gave me Godly, wise counsel as I navigated through the ugly divorce process. She was one of my few friends who "knew" way before the darkness in our marriage was exposed. The Lord had shown her. She had been praying for me for years and was ready when all the darkness came out. I came to her for guidance. Nothing binds you more than going through tragedy together.

By the time all the divorce proceedings were in full force, I looked like a hot mess. I had lost 15 pounds (the great divorce diet), my hair had turned completely white on the top of my head, and it was falling out, and my skin color was literally a gray tone. Not only did I look, as they say in Texas, "ridden hard and put up wet," but I also had a hard time concentrating on tasks, which didn't help when you're already a little ADD. Every day, I would receive over 20 pages of attorney jargon. I came to believe that divorce proceedings are all a ploy to get women like me just to throw in the towel and scream, "I surrender! Where do I sign?" The opposite side just tries to inundate you with information you don't understand and to wear you down until you are so weary that you don't care anymore. Every day, I felt like giving up and giving in. But inevitably, my stubborn genes would assert themselves. I refused to be defeated.

Not only did I have pages and pages of papers to read, but I had to look up facts and terminologies to refute the pages and pages. I was so shocked that my marriage had been reduced to pages of "who gets what." In a nutshell, once we were in the divorce proceedings, my husband was done with our relationship. He had moved on. The divorce process is nothing but a business transaction. Once you get to the divorce proceedings, it's just a game of how much an individual must fork over, no matter the contributions.

How do you separate 25 years of "stuff?" After all, that was never my plan. If someone had told me even one day before the crash, I wouldn't have believed it. I was overwhelmed. I couldn't even focus enough to read the Bible–the very thing I needed the most. I resorted to downloading The Word, sermons from great men and women of God, and worship music on my iPod. I basically became Forrest Gump. I couldn't stay in that empty house alone. And I certainly didn't want to take my married friends away from their families and busy lives. So, I walked and walked and walked. As I walked, I cried out to God, "Help!" Sometimes, that's about all I could get out.

During that period of two years, I was desperate. All I knew to do was walk and fill myself with truth. That was my only solace, besides probably driving my friends crazy with all the divorce stuff. Every day, I would put those exercise clothes on, take my iPod loaded with truth, and take my Starbucks or Coffee Bean card (depending on my mood), and off I went. Some days, I prayed for guidance. Some days, I would fall to the ground and cry. And some days, I wanted to smack the livin' daylights out of Michael. I was going for the "righteous anger," but I don't think God was buying that strategy. "Vengeance is Mine," says the Lord.

One of my best friends, Monsita, and I would walk in the mornings together. She patiently listened to me rant and rave. Then we would pray together. What a loyal friend she has always been. I'm not sure I could have patiently listened to me during those times. I was the poster child for James 3:9 (NKJV), "With it (the tongue) we bless our God and Father, and with it, we curse men, who have been made in the similitude of God." My mouth was (and still can be) unruly. Yet another thing to work on. I had so many friends who were there for me and loved me despite myself. There's no way I could ever thank them enough.

I can vividly recall one morning when Monsita and I went for our walk and coffee. When we got back to the house, the electric gates wouldn't open. The gates were eight feet tall. I couldn't climb them if I wanted to. I couldn't get into the property, and Monsita couldn't get her car. A minute later, a man came walking out of the gate. I saw an electric company emblem on his shirt. You can imagine how thrilled I was to see him. I explained I couldn't get the gate to open. He replied that he had an order to turn the electricity off on the property. As I stood there, tears started running down my face, yet another blow. That was just cruel. I confessed to him I was going through a divorce, and I didn't know what to do. He looked at me and said, "Ma'am, I've seen this before. I'm going to go back in and turn your electricity back on and speak with my manager and make sure you have three months to sort things out before anything is turned off." How God takes care of His children!

Monsita and I marveled at the Lord's timing. Had we been one minute later, we would have missed the serviceman. Had we sat and sipped our lattes just a few more minutes, we would have been stranded for who knows how many more hours or days before the electric company could get back out to the house. That kind man showed me mercy. I have heard people say, "God doesn't part the Red Sea anymore." I beg to differ. He parts the Red Sea for me every single day. It was the gates that day, but nothing short of a miracle.

Two years later, with the divorce almost finalized, I put our Beverly Hills home on the market. My Godmother, Jean (the one I ran to in Aspen when my world first came crashing down), was staying with me. She was housebound after having double knee replacement surgery. When I got a call for a showing, I explained to the realtor that we would have to be in the house during the showing, but we would try to stay out of the way. A beautiful Indian couple came through the house. The man, a prominent Bollywood producer, looked shocked when he saw me. "YOU live here?" he asked. "Yes." "So, this is your mother's home, and you live with her?" he continued, referring to Jean. "No, this is my home (that the Lord had loaned me), and my Godmother is staying with me while she recuperates from surgery," I said. Even more astonished, he asked, "Wait … this is your home?"

I had no idea why this puzzled him so.

With a huge sigh, he said, "I am so relieved this is your home. I see you walking everywhere—Beverly Hills, West Hollywood, Brentwood, Santa Monica. I've seen you talking to yourself (that would be me praying) and raising your hands (that would be me praising the Lord, "raise up holy hands unto the Lord"). I am so relieved that you have a home."

Now I've been called a lot of things in my life–church lady, holy roller, "she's a very religious person," and more, but being called homeless was a new one. I really needed to get my stuff together. Like Forrest Gump, we all occasionally need a wake-up call and realize we can never run away from our problems. I love the saying, "If you're going through hell, don't stop." I was going through hell, and I refused to stop. I was relentless with God, and I was not going to stop until He healed my hammered heart. There are no shortcuts in healing or mourning. I had to gut it out.

Apparently, in the hours I spent trudging the city of Los Angeles, I truly did look like Ellie May Clampett from *The Beverly Hillbillies*. We all have different ways of going through the healing process, and that one just seemed to work for me. I also believe physical activity is also good for our mental health. It certainly worked as a part of my healing process.

As I look back, I marvel at how God guided me, even with my finances. God cares about our finances because He cares about our well-being. His plan for our lives is not to survive but to thrive. Another lesson I was about to witness.

Let's pray together

Jesus, I was relentless for my healing, as I know You relentlessly pursue Your children. There is no true healing without You. You showed me grace, and You did it! I know You with all my heart. I Thank you for being my Father and my Friend. Amen

Chapter 13

Apple

God is always guiding me and giving me wisdom. That was so evident when He put a stock on my mind. I didn't know much about the stock market, except you're supposed to buy low and sell high. This stock ended up saving me. God came through for me in the most practical ways because He is a practical God.

I have always relied on the Lord, but now that I am divorced and single, I need Him even more. For 25 years of my marriage, I thought life was free. I never saw a bill, never made a plane reservation, and had no idea how to keep records of paying taxes, which health insurance to go with, how to get car insurance, license tag renewals, passports, etc. I just signed every document put in front of me. Maybe not the smartest thing I've ever done, but hindsight is 20/20. When asked in the deposition why I would sign documents I didn't read, my response was, "My mom can trust my dad. That's all I have ever known. And why would I be married to a man I didn't trust?"

I never gave finances much thought. Not only that, but I was also a working mom and renovated countless homes, which took a lot of concentration. Well, that gravy train stopped in an instant. The next thing I knew, bank accounts were closed, and credit cards were canceled. It was like someone stabbed me with a knife. At the time, I didn't even know the name of our banker. While Michael was buying cars freely, I was put on an "expense account" during our mediation process. I felt like I was in school again when I had an allowance. It was totally demoralizing. I began selling off my jewelry to pay legal fees.

That's when the Lord stepped up to the plate once again, and miracles happened. I remember my first Christmas alone, and all our accounts were closed. I couldn't even buy my sons and their spouses gifts. I certainly didn't want to go to my parents for help. I somehow thought in the back of my mind that this was only temporary and everything would be okay. Because of that, I did not want to let my family know everything that was happening to me just in case there was a chance

Michael and I would get back together. My family would forgive, but they would have a hard time forgetting. So, there I was again, trying to figure things out on my own. The day before I left to go to Dallas for Christmas with my parents, sisters, and their families, God brought our private banker to my remembrance. I called him in desperation. Typically, a banker would continue with the client who had the most business in their bank, not the floundering spouse, who would most likely end up with much less capital. Nonetheless, our banker, Jeffrey, took compassion on me. I had no idea what to expect when I called. All I knew was I had one day before I got on that plane, and this was my only shot. I called to arrange a meeting. His secretary said he was in meetings all day but would try to get him to call me back. It was not looking good. I watched the time crawl by. Then the phone rang. Jeffrey said he had a 20-minute break if I could be at his office at 3:00 p.m. He was already aware of our accounts being closed and figured out what was happening (this wasn't his first rodeo). I walked into his office looking like something the cat had dragged in after not sleeping a wink the night before. He kindly sat me down and said how sorry he was to learn about my situation. He said he had watched me for many years renovating houses and having success. I did make a big contribution to the marriage. Those projects became God's provision to take care of me for the rest of my life. God knew something I didn't know.

Jeffrey reviewed our portfolio and said, "I'm not going to tell you what to do, but if I were you, this is what I would do." Then he advised me on what "he" would do because there was an account that hadn't been touched in years. He became like a concerned big brother. Jeffrey was the answer to my prayer, but I knew it was God who came through in the eleventh hour.

Looking back, I should have written Michael a thank you note. It was times like these that gave me such a passion to help women who have been abandoned and left with nothing while trying to support children and take care of themselves. I certainly didn't know what to do, and although my situation was short-lived, I now knew the desperate feeling of not knowing if I was going to make it or not. God never wastes a hurt. That's more than just a nice thing to stitch on a pillow.

God also began to prepare another way for me to survive five years before everything came crashing down. My dad had always bought stocks for his three girls and grandchildren for our future. My dad, the epitome of the conservative banker, always bought the blue chip, conservative stocks. He used to say, "I made my money a little bit at a time, so if I'm going to lose some, I'm going to lose it a little bit at a time." He was not a big risk-taker. You can imagine his response when I called him one day in 2003 and told him I had just bought my first iPod. "Dad! This new iPod I have is the greatest thing ever. You won't believe the technology and how easy it is to use." I told my dad, "I want you to please sell all the stocks you gave me, and I want to buy all Apple stock." There was a long pause on the other line. Then I heard, "Now honey, you don't want to put all your eggs in one basket." He asked me about how the company was doing. I knew nada about the company, only how much better the iPod was next to my old Walkman or the Discman–both of which skipped a beat sometimes when you were running. Not to mention, you could only play one cassette or disc at a time on those devices. The iPod played hundreds of songs, and I could jump off a building, and it wouldn't skip. I adored this new gadget that was making my workouts much more fun. I knew I couldn't be the only one amazed with this tiny square. Disgruntled, my dad finally sold all my stocks so I could purchase Apple.

When the divorce crash came, I was miserable staying in that big house in Beverly Hills all alone. I remember walking through the streets of Beverly Hills, wondering how many of us women were living in these big homes, looking like we had everything yet were miserable.

I needed to get away. Yet I didn't have the money to even book a flight. Then I remembered the Apple stock I had bought. I never really paid attention to how the stock was doing, but after the first iPhone came out in 2007, it went through the roof. I had no idea how much the revolutionary iPhone and MacBook would make the stock soar. But God did. He gave me the idea to purchase stock in a company I knew nothing about, and that stock would help me in my future when I had no income stream at the beginning of the divorce proceedings.

When I was in Dallas with my family, I realized I needed a "cocoon," a safe place to go near my family and in the Bible belt. Dallas, like Tulsa, is the buckle of the Bible belt. While there for that first Christmas alone, I walked into a store and heard gospel music. Right then, I thought, this is where I belong. Nowhere in Los Angeles would you walk into a commercial store with gospel music playing.

I needed to be in Dallas. But how could I afford a move? APPLE! The stock God blessed me with got me a temporary loan, using it as collateral (I certainly wasn't going to sell any of the stock since it kept climbing upward) to buy a condo in Dallas. I called it my "jewel box"— truly a gift from Him. I spent a lot of time with my family and my wonderful new church, Upperroom, which became my safe haven and healing place. On a side note, it has been suggested not to make any big decisions after divorce or spousal loss for at least two years. Well, I blew that theory out of the water. But thankfully, God wanted to heal my heart in my new church in Dallas and be with my original family. He provided a healing sanctuary so I could be restored and hopefully forgive and be able to help others going through the same devastation.

Some people get upset and say, "God doesn't care about your businesses or how much money you make." I beg to differ. I love the Bible verse, "We are blessed to be a blessing." I've already said, "The gospel is free, but ministry is expensive." Jesus paid the price, and all we have to do is ask Jesus to be the Lord of our lives, and it is done. That's a gift. However, sharing that truth with the world through different ministries is costly. It costs money to run a church, pay the employees, and pay all the daily expenses. It costs money to send missionaries out into the world "to spread the gospel." I believe God blesses people to be a blessing so we can support missionaries who sacrifice their lives for the gospel and tithe to our churches to keep them running.

I must say, I don't think for one minute that Michael was the only one to blame. Sometimes, I was like a stubborn kindergartner. It takes two to tango and two to "untango." I wish I could tell you I always did my part and did the right thing when God kept showing up on my behalf, but I didn't. When I was about to move some of my things from the Beverly Hills house to Dallas after purchasing the condo, someone ratted on me and told Michael I was going to move things out. A letter from his attorney was hand-delivered to me saying I was in contempt of court. It was against the law to move possessions out of the state until the divorce was settled and all the personal property was properly divided. He had already come into the house and put post-it notes all around it, taken everything he wanted, and moved them to our—now his—home in Montecito. I felt free to take some of the furniture to Dallas. Why would he want the hot pink and lime green furniture anyway? He left that furniture behind. But it's all about wanting you to wave the white flag of surrender in divorce. I felt beaten down, but that didn't last. I picked up the phone and dialed the moving company. "There are some new circumstances, and I will need a 40-foot truck instead of the original 20-foot truck I originally ordered first thing in the morning. Oh, and have a great day."

I am not proud of this incident (and several more), but I quite enjoyed it at the time. But that doesn't make it right. I just knew I had to get to Texas and make it home. And you know what they say: don't mess with Texas.

Our hearts are always on a journey. Forgiveness and finding wholeness have been a process. Grief can still come out of nowhere.

I had purchased a condo in Dallas after my divorce. One day, I was on a morning walk and was passing my friends Jeanne and Barry's house. We raised our children together and have many memories of traveling as families. I had to adjust to the fact that I was not a "couple" anymore, and sadly, it hit me that we wouldn't be raising our grandchildren together as couples.

I decided to reach out and rang Jeanne's doorbell. As she opened the door, I was suddenly bawling like a baby. My emotions were all over the place. Dallas was proving to be a good place for me to recover from my heartbreak.

Tigger and Leo were also very close Dallas friends and showed me great compassion for my new reality as a suddenly single person. Tigger always makes me laugh. I'm so grateful for their friendship. Tigger stood by my side during my mediation and I will never forget it. Friends like these have been a lifeline to me.

Let's pray together

Jesus, when I walked down that aisle to get married, I certainly didn't think,   Maybe this will work, maybe this won t." But I know people have free will and choice. I don t like how this ended, but one thing I know is You are faithful. You step in and help us. Thank you for that when people fail us. Amen

Chapter 14

Conversations with God

Yes, I do question God. I never once in my life questioned His Lordship. I just questioned why things were happening to me. Oh, the conversations I have had with Him. Looking back, I see how irrational I was when I got knocked off my feet. Even though it wasn't God who caused all this, I seemed to blame Him for letting it happen. But this was not God doing anything to me. This was the failure of man.

Having many years under my belt, I have seen and heard from some of the best people in the world who suffered terribly from someone close to them who allowed darkness to creep into their lives. One story that strongly comes to my mind is the life of Corrie Ten Boom. She and her family hid many Jews in the attic and basement of their home and kept them from being taken and killed by the Nazis. Because of this heroic stance, Corrie and her entire family were eventually found out and sent to concentration camps. Corrie had to stand in line next to her sister for hours, weakened and tortured by the Nazi guards in the camp. One day, her sister fell, exhausted by the hours of forced labor, illness, and starvation. Corrie watched her sister beaten to death by a Nazi female prison guard. During her Nazi concentration camp years, amongst the other prisoners, she shared the gospel from a tiny Bible she smuggled in. After Corrie was released from the concentration camp, she became a minister for Christ and traveled all over the world sharing the forgiving love of Jesus. Decades later, Corrie was speaking one evening in Europe when a woman came forward and answered an altar call to accept Jesus into her heart as her Lord and Savior. That very woman was the Nazi prison guard who had beaten her sister to death. Corrie internally cried out to God when she recognized her and said, "Lord, this is asking too much of me. I can't forgive this woman."

Jesus, in His beautiful, still voice, said to her, "I will help you forgive her." Corrie took her hand and prayed with this woman to accept Jesus into her heart. That's the power of God in our lives. He can forgive and minister, especially to this prison guard who took so much from Corrie's life.

I learned of Corrie's story from a wonderful book by Eric Metaxas, "Seven Women." Every one of the seven women he wrote about changed the world they lived in for Christ. Yet, all of them endured extreme persecution and horrible afflictions. I think of how their faithful ministries cost them everything, and I mean everything. However, generations were changed because of their stance on spreading the gospel through the love of Jesus.

Corrie had a stroke in the last years of her life. She was housebound and suffered for several years. After devoting her life to ministering the gospel, it's so easy to ask, "God, why did this happen to such an amazing woman who gave her life and all for You?" In man's finite mind, it seems so unfair. It's easy to question God why so many good people suffer in this life. The Bible tells us suffering doesn't come from God. We live in a hurting world and "hurt people, hurt people." God is a good God; He wants the very best for His children like we do for our own children. Good things happen to bad people, and bad things happen to good people. As a parent, I know my children have and will go through times of suffering. I pray I can always be there for them, just as Jesus is always there for us. From those trials, we grow.

What I have learned is I grow exponentially in bad times and seem to sail along in a mediocre state in good times. I also don't think God is to blame for humans 'poor decisions. There are always consequences for me when I make dumb choices. But He is always there with open arms to welcome me back into the fold. The same goes for you, too.

I look at how Jesus restored my life, whether emotionally, physically, or financially. I've learned that without Him my life would be futile. I have always lived for Jesus, but now I have totally devoted my life to Christ. I have seen countless people come to Jesus in the last few years. Many people were healed. To be completely clear, I have seen none of these things on my account. I can't heal or "fix" anyone's life. I simply share Jesus 'love on the streets, in Uber rides (I mean, where can the driver go?), at restaurants, galas, speaking engagements, dinner parties, and airplanes. I just pray everywhere I go that Jesus will sit me next to the very person who is hurting and needs Him. I can share this with such compassion because I have experienced and understand loss and devastation on a first-name basis.

I think of the day Corrie met her Savior and how all the angels and loved ones must have rejoiced as she entered heaven. I guarantee that she didn't question God about the suffering she or her loved ones had to go through on that day. She knew all the suffering in the world was worth all the souls who came to know Him through her beautiful ministry. When I am face-to-face with my Savior, I will not look back and say, "Well, that wasn't worth the cost of my losses here on Earth." I will worship and praise my Savior and say, "It was worth it all." Now, that's a conversation I'm looking forward to having.

Let's pray together

Lord, we learn to trust You when we hit rock bottom, and You are always there. Out of the ten lepers who were healed, help me always be reminded of all You have done for me, so I am that one leper who returns to give You glory and say   thanks!" Amen

Chapter 15

Hammered Heart

After two years of brutal divorce proceedings, I was worn out. I needed Him to "make good" on His promise of healing me. That meant there was work to be done on my part, like that dreaded word forgiveness. And He did heal my heart in the very place where He died thousands of years ago.

My dear friends Emilie and Craig planned a trip to Israel for a small group of us to walk where Jesus walked. Kathie Lee and Frank helped put the small, intimate group together, and many amazing friendships that will last a lifetime came out of that trip. At the time, I was in the thick of my divorce and didn't know if I could get away. I knew I needed to go. Sure enough, another miracle happened. Our final divorce mediation was set for 10 days before I was to leave for Israel. I was desperate to go, but I didn't want to leave if things were still unsettled. I started praying for "Godspeed." The two previous mediations were ruthless. I left with my tail between my legs with no settlement even close to a resolution. If we couldn't settle the third time, we would have to go to court. Who knows how long or how much more money that would cost? This moment was crucial. There seemed to be a wide divide about the amount my worth in the marriage would cost Michael. However, I had to pay him the king's ransom from the real estate profits God blessed me with during those 25 years. This was the result of the papers I had signed. Again, note to self: don't sign anything you don't read. The Lord blessed my businesses of renovating properties during our marriage. He helped me create my own stability. Yet, for some reason, my husband didn't think I was even worthy of those funds. I later learned it was more about punishing me for having the audacity to leave.

Michael had a whole other value of my "worth." Every day, I kept asking the Lord to let us come to an agreement and stop the madness so I could get on that plane to Israel as a free woman.

Ask, and you shall receive. God doesn't just handle the what and the when. He has always been faithful to me in bringing the who. That was a friend of mine who is married to a federal judge. Little did I know her husband would be so pinnacle to me during the divorce proceedings. After all, who knows more about the law than a federal judge?

During the divorce drama, I was visiting them for dinner one weekend up in Montecito. As I was telling my friend's husband, Terry, everything I was going through, he stopped me (as I can be a little long-winded) and said, "Your problem is you're too nice, and you're allowing his team of attorneys to bully you. You need to go watch the movie 'Mean Girls' and get mean." I learned that nice doesn't get you a fair shake in a divorce.

He went on to explain the battle tactic during our dinner. I was instructed to walk into the boardroom, not say too much, and present the plan of basically what I would accept. Then, don't say another word. Finally, Terry instructed, "If they don't agree with your terms, get up and say, 'We are done 'and walk out."

He said they would come chasing me down the hallway. That was all the advice he gave me. I've always said not to ask for people's advice if you aren't going to take it and not to ask for advice from people who don't know what they are talking about. Terry knew what he was talking about.

As for the advice, I took it. I prayed about it for two weeks. I woke up on the morning of the final mediation and prayed some more. I opened my Bible Russian roulette-style—just open it and see what jumped out at me. Amazingly, I went straight to this verse: "Today is your day in court, take your strongest argument." (Isaiah 41:21)

Can I get a witness? I couldn't get over it, dumbfounded at the grace of God. This was the day I would be free from living under all this darkness.

I put my fatigues (armor of God) on and went for it. Doing what I was instructed, I made what I felt was a fair proposal: take it or leave it. I got up and walked out. Just like Terry said, they came walking—well, practically running—down the hallway after me to bring me back in. That's when we made the deal. I am eternally grateful to both of my friends. That dinner was a divine appointment. Once again, God's sovereign timing of my friends being in California for the summer, inviting me to dinner, and giving me sound, knowledgeable advice changed the course of my life.

"A wise man will hear and increase in learning, and a man of understanding will acquire wise counsel." (Proverbs 1:5, NKJV) God set the entire thing up for me. I didn't drive up to Montecito thinking I was going up to seek counsel. I was just going to have dinner with old friends from my hometown. But God had a much bigger plan.

Miraculously, we settled that day. It was finally over. Or so I thought.

After everything was signed, sealed, and delivered, I asked my attorney, Nan, "So, it's done?" She said, "Yes, it is finalized. However, you are not legally divorced until the papers are sent downtown, and it is signed off by the judge and recorded."

I know this gets down to logistics, but in my mind, I needed it recorded in the court system as legally over. I needed finality. I replied, "So, this will take a few days. Then will it be done?"

Nan said that since the California court system is backlogged, it usually takes four to six weeks for everything to go through. "That doesn't work for me at all," I said. "I need you to please have someone drive the papers down and get them recorded. I have been praying for a miracle that this divorce would be finalized before I step foot on that plane for Israel, which is in five days. I need to be free to move forward with my healing." She looked at me like I was joking and said, "Well, that's impossible. I have never seen it happen in a few days in my years of practicing law. It's out of our control and in the court system's hands."

Well, let's just see about that. On my knees I went.

Three business days later, Nan called me, astounded. "I can't even believe this. Your papers have been signed and recorded. You are a free woman." She reiterated how she had never seen this happen before in such a short time. Another miracle!

I began rejoicing, thanking and praising the Lord right there on the phone. At that point, I knew the Lord was going to work on my hammered heart. I just didn't know when.

Before we left on the trip, we were instructed to start walking eight miles a day to prepare for all the hiking we would be doing. "Forrest Gump" was ready. No prep needed. We were sent a backpack with items and a list of things we needed to bring, like hiking shoes, hats, and a roll of toilet paper... wait a minute, you lost me there. A roll of toilet paper? Why in the world would you need a roll of toilet paper in your backpack? I soon learned. When you are hiking out in the desert in the caves of Ein Gedi, where David feared for his life at the hands of King Saul, there aren't restrooms with Dyson hand dryers. Any preconceived rules you like to live by are thrown out the window when you are out in the middle of the desert with friends. If passing a roll of toilet paper around doesn't bond you for life, nothing will.

The Israelis amaze me. They are and have had to be, very resilient people. There are some simple observances beyond the history of our Messiah that I got a kick out of. One day, we were on a bus at the top of a mountain range (first, who takes a bus to the top of a mountain in the middle of the desert?) I am not talking about paved roads. I'm talking about desert roads with huge rocks and boulders. I had to fight car and bus sickness the entire way as we rocked back and forth on the way up and down, but the trip was worth it. We were where Mary and Joseph walked miles and miles back from Jerusalem after Passover. Mary was probably either barefoot or in leather sandals. She had no energy drinks, protein bars, or New Balance hiking shoes. They got halfway home through the mountain ranges and had to go back because Jesus had been left behind preaching in the synagogue. It's a good thing I wasn't Mary having to walk all the way back. Jesus would have gotten the "What in the world were you thinking?" speech. I guess He was thinking of the world!

I was struggling just on the bus ride, much less making that journey walking in those conditions as Mary had. As we neared the top of the mountain, I realized how important and strategic the Gaza Strip is. Out of nowhere, my cell phone started ringing. For crying out loud, I lived in Beverly Hills, and we had to have special cell towers installed on our roof to get reception. And their military? Forget about it. I loved seeing the small girls around 17 years old walking around in military fatigues carrying huge machine guns that weighed as much as they did. All high school graduates must serve one year in the military. Now that is legit. I have never felt safer in my life than when I was in Israel. I wouldn't want to, nor should we, go to war with Israel. They will beat us. I've read the back of the Book!

Biblically, God says of Israel, "I will bless those who bless you, and curse those who curse you." (Genesis 12:3, NKJV) In the new covenant/testament, that includes all of us who believe in the one true God. The only difference is most Jews believe their Messiah is coming, and the Christians believe Jesus is the Messiah. We, as Christians, are grafted into the original covenant the Lord made with the Israelites. If a Christian reads and studies the Bible and loves God, then it is impossible to be antisemitic. We can see how the devil uses certain extremist groups of religions to try to kill and destroy other religions. We can hate what extremists "do." God says, "Hate evil, you who love the Lord, who preserves the soul of His godly ones; He delivers." But we are not called to hate mankind.

In the first four days, we experienced the Bible come alive. Standing on the shores of Galilee was incredible, where Jesus told Matthew and Peter to cast out their nets after catching nothing the night before. I could envision them drawing up the net with so many fish that the nets started to tear. Our bible scholar, Ray, who studied at Hebrew University, taught us how to understand the Word of God from the Middle Eastern Jewish culture that Jesus and all his Jewish disciples were raised in. By the time we came back to the hotel at night, we were filthy and mentally exhausted. We all could not get over the information overload. I mean, most of us thought we knew the Word pretty well. It was one of the most humbling experiences I've ever had, realizing how little I really knew. But during that time, Jesus was teaching me and enveloping me with Ray's teachings.

I was also being reached on a personal level. Several other women on this trip had gone through their own trials of infidelity. Kathie Lee, Emilie, Lesley, Tina, Karen, Laurie, and Martha took me under their wings and taught me what the root word "compassion" means–to "suffer with." The root word of "excruciating" means "out of the cross." Jesus gave me friends to "suffer with," friends who had also gone through the pain I was going through. They understood the devastation. Jesus went to the cross for us, the worst possible way to die, so my suffering and excruciating pain would be healed in Him. He handpicked these beautiful women who were Godly and there for me on this trip. At our ages, none of us were unscathed from major trials. Every heart has been hammered in one way or another. They all encouraged me that the Lord has a "future and a hope for me," even if I felt hopeless.

Being in such an amazing place, with beautiful friends and my divorce finally final, I thought I would feel alive and free, but it was the opposite. I really noticed this numbness when we were in the Garden of Gethsemane. There were people from all over the world, and many were singing songs of praise in their own languages. How could anyone not be moved by the experience? Well, I wasn't. I was stone cold. I could not show or experience any emotion, which was unusual for me. I had let my heart get hardened as a defense mechanism. It was my way of coping with all the pain of being beaten down emotionally and the feeling of rejection by the man I thought was my soulmate.

Toward the end of our trip, we went to Caesarea, where Paul stood trial before King Herod for preaching the gospel in synagogues. I was standing exactly where Paul stood thousands of years before. Amongst the crowds, they were all yelling for him to be killed for preaching Jesus as the Messiah, which was pure blasphemy in the Pharisees' eyes. I was standing in the ruins of Herod's Decapolis just imagining this scene.

Herod was known to be a prolific architect and designer. There were gorgeous marble mosaic floors and ancient marble columns imported from Italy. The Lord knows how to get my attention; I'm an architectural freak and love beauty. As I was marveling at the incredible ruins, I looked down and saw a little heart-shaped stone at my feet. It wasn't a commercialized perfect heart but an asymmetrical, contemporary-styled heart that looked like a jeweler had hammered it. I picked up the small stone. As I held it in my hand, I had a "God moment." It felt like warm oil was pouring over me, starting from the top of my head all the way down to my feet. Then, it felt like huge arms were wrapped around me. For the first time in a long while, I felt safe. As I looked at the stone in my hand, these words came to me, "I will take your heart of stone, and I will turn it to flesh, and I am going to heal your heart."

Right at that moment, the floodgates opened, and my emotions began coming back. I later realized He spoke to me from Ezekiel 36:26-27 (NKJV), which says, "I will give you a new heart and put a new spirit within you; I will take the heart of stone out of your flesh and give you a heart of flesh. I will put My spirit within you and cause you to walk in My statutes, and you will keep My judgments and do them."

I was so moved. I began sobbing tears that I needed to shed for two pent-up years. Those tears turned to tears of joy. I knew Jesus had used that little rock to "show up" and reveal Himself to me so I would know that He was going to not only take care of me, but we were going to thrive together! I went from survival mode to thriving mode. We can't ever give up because our situations can change in an instant. The Bible talks about "suddenlies" when things can change on a dime. I hate to think of us giving up right before God was about to change our lives instantaneously, just as He did for me in that moment. I say to you, don't ever give up. Timing is not ours. It's the Lord's.

I had to leave the Israel trip a few days earlier than our group because my son Viktor was graduating from Pepperdine. That event would be the first time I would be put into a social setting with Michael since we separated, apart from the attorney's boardroom when we were on opposite sides of the table. At that graduation, it was obvious that Jesus had given me a new heart on my trip. When I saw Michael, I told him how sorry I was that things had gotten so ugly and asked him to please forgive me for anything I did to hurt him. Before Israel, I would have thought he should apologize to me. Michael responded with the same ask of forgiveness for the hurtful things he had done to me. I found out later that Viktor was so nervous the night before the graduation ceremony that he didn't sleep a wink. He didn't know how it would be with both his parents there together for the first time after a hurtful divorce. When he saw us hug and being so friendly together, not to mention hosting a luncheon afterward, I realized that this forgiveness was not only for each other, but also for our sons. Note to parents: the greatest gift you can give your children besides loving God, each other, and them, is to forgive. After that graduation, Michael and I became friends and shared many holidays together with our children and grandchildren.

Following Viktor's graduation, I went back home to Los Angeles and put the stone next to my bedside. Life went on as usual, but I was free. Thankfully, I had Jewels.

She had no idea when she had come to work for us three years earlier that my life would crash and burn after just six months of working with me. Jewels had her hands full getting me up to speed.

One Sunday, I remember taking my girls from the Dream Center out for breakfast before church. When the bill came, I called her in a panic. I had switched purses and forgot my wallet in the other purse, the days before Apple Pay. Jewels said she was already downtown at the church and didn't have any cash on her, but she could go to an ATM and get cash for me. I replied, "Jewels, it's Sunday. The banks are closed. We can't get any cash. What am I going to do?" There was a long pause. Then, she finally said, "Don't ever tell anyone you said that to me." Apparently, those machines are open 24/7. Who knew?! In the past, Michael had always been my ATM and kept cash in his green jacket. Yet another learning curve.

Jewels constantly had to pick up the pieces from the messes I would get myself in. It was like taking care of Lucy from the *I Love Lucy* show. We were out running errands one day, and I got a flat tire. It was rush hour in Beverly Hills, and I wasn't having it. Sitting and waiting for AAA just didn't seem to work for me. I told Jewels, "Let's just clump, clump this baby into the dealership, so we don't have to wait for the tow truck."

Jewels was the practical one who said, "No way! It will ruin your rim." At that moment, I didn't care. I just didn't want to wait hours for the tow truck. We clumped to the dealership, laughing at how ridiculous we looked going ten miles per hour with my car thumping. As they were fixing the flat tire, we were drinking cappuccinos at the dealership and watching a football game. Suddenly, I had that same "God moment" like I had in Israel. That warmth came over me and God spoke to me in that still-small "knowing." He said, "Dru, when you get a flat tire, it's an inconvenience; when many other divorced women get a flat tire, it's catastrophic. They can't afford a tow truck or new tires. Then, they can't get their children to school and get to work. It's a spiral effect for them. I gave you that heart for a reason, to help women."

I knew it was God speaking to me. I'm not smart enough to come up with the idea He gave me. I took the stone to my sister Mel, who is a jeweler. She had a cast made of the stone, and we began casting it into yellow, white and rose gold, silver, and pavé diamond. I sent one to Emilie and Kathie Lee to thank them for taking me on the Israel trip. I shared how the Lord had given me a new passion for helping women who were struggling financially through divorce and abandonment—all a result of the trip they planned.

Kathie Lee put the heart on the Today Show as one of her "favorite things." I began selling them, but mostly donating the diamond hearts to Christian ministries and charities to sell at their events and annual galas. All the proceeds go directly to help women and children. I began giving the diamond pave hearts to all the Childhelp events and their annual gala. I also gave them to a wonderful ministry called Mercy Multiplied for their annual galas and other ministries and churches. I'm always astounded how sometimes the necklaces can go for up to ten times my cost base and sell in multiples. One hundred percent of the money raised goes directly to charities, which in turn can disperse money to help struggling and hurting women, single parents, and children. It's all by the grace of God that I have the privilege of traveling around, speaking at events, and sharing how the Lord miraculously gave me this ministry. Men get in bidding wars over my diamond hearts because their wives are kicking them under the table. After all, supposedly, a diamond is a girl's best friend. Best of all, I get to watch how the Lord took my devastating divorce, taught me to forgive, and allowed me to bless ministries so they can help women and children who are heartbroken and destitute. God gave me the Hammered Heart Foundation and turned my lemons into lemonade!

Let's pray together

Jesus, You turned my heartache into healing. You took my heart of stone and softened it and turned it into a heart of flesh that can hear You and forgive, even when I didn't want to. Thanks to You, I can now turn my hurt for good to help others who have been hammered by life. Amen

Chapter 16

God's Unfolding Mysteries

There have been periods of my life when I had God on a shelf. I never left Him but didn't "dwell in Him." I would bring Him into my life when I needed Him, then put Him right back on that shelf when life began to run smoothly again. The good part is I have grown much more in tough times. I'm the first one to cry out to God for help. But when the storms pass, I'm off with a busy life again. As they say, "If the devil can't get you bad, he will get you busy."

There are times I think that I'm too busy to read the Bible every day. Yet I find it amazing how I seem to be able to squeeze it in when I need a miracle.

After my divorce, I bought a condo in Dallas because I wanted to be closer to my sisters and parents. At least, I thought that was why I moved to Dallas. In hindsight, I know exactly why God moved mountains for me in providing the space in Dallas. I had to learn a great lesson on how to draw closer to Him. I would venture to say we all know people who when you see their phone call coming in you send it to voicemail immediately. You just have to be "in the mood" to take that call. You know it won't be a five-minute conversation because those certain individuals will go on for an hour, and it's usually a one-way conversation. You can't get a word in edgewise. Well, I realized I was one of "those people" when it came to my relationship with God. I would be driving around playing worship music and praying to God with that eternal list of what I needed Him to do for me. It was a lot like whining and complaining that life wasn't exactly the way I thought it should be.

Here's what my prayers were: First, I would thank God for being so good to me and my family. Then, ask Him to forgive all my sins, as there are many, and then proceed to tell Him how much I loved Him. After that, the list would start. I would list everything I needed Him to do for me. Next, I would profusely thank Him for taking care of my list. Only to restart those same prayers over and over and over again.

Where would we be without family and friends? After the divorce, I got a call from one of my best friends, Nancy, who is like a sister to me, and her husband got on the phone and said, "We know who is to fault here, but I want to know if it's ok if I remain friends with Michael because I think he needs a true friend right now as he seems to be spiraling."

I said, "Jim, I would never want you to have to choose sides, and I'm begging you to remain friends. He needs Christian friends, and you are his best friend." The same thing happened with so many of our couple friends. Julie was my comic relief friend. She made me laugh when I wanted to cry; laughter is indeed the best medicine.

I always thought I had this healthy relationship with God. I read the Bible, went to Bible studies, worked with hurting women, prayed, ministered to people, and taught my children the ways of the Lord. Then, two very pinnacle things happened that would change the course of my prayer life and the way I saw God.

After I moved to Dallas, I flew to Scottsdale to help with an amazing organization called Childhelp. Childhelp was founded by Sara O'Meara and Yvonne Fedderson, two of the wisest women I know. I call them "my mamas." They have devoted their entire lives to helping abused children. They started Childhelp over 65 years ago and counting. Both women were actresses and went to Tokyo to entertain our troops overseas. Just like me in Dallas, they thought they were going to Tokyo for one reason. But Jesus changed the course of their trip, not to mention the whole course of their lives. When they arrived in Japan, there was a typhoon so intense they couldn't leave their hotel room for three days.

After they couldn't take being cooped up any longer, they put on rain galoshes, grabbed umbrellas, and just went out to walk around town. They found children on the streets who were homeless, soaking wet and freezing. Some were as young as babies and were being cared for by children too young to have such a huge responsibility. Sara and Yvonne found out that these children were abandoned because they were children of mixed heritage, Japanese and American, thanks to servicemen having a good time. In the Japanese culture at that time, unwed pregnancy was a huge disgrace for women, not to mention those of mixed heritages. Therefore, they would abandon the children on the streets. Sara and Yvonne were appalled and couldn't get those precious children off their minds. They ended up bringing as many babies as they could back to their hotel room and had them sleeping on every inch of their beds and floor. They fed them and then turned to the servicemen to help pitch in and feed and clothe them. At that moment, they realized they had a much higher calling and committed the rest of their lives to save children from abuse and abandonment. They didn't leave Japan until they found a place for those children. By the time they were ready to leave, they discovered hundreds of children in crisis. They found a tiny orphanage there and refused to leave until they raised enough money to support all the children, even adding on to the home to make room for more children who were left on the streets.

Originally, the orphanage had two tiny rooms. There was no door and open windows in the freezing cold, and only a hibachi was in each room for partial warmth. Hanging on two hooks were two ragged, tiny coats that the children had to share when they went outside. That's all those two ladies had to see. That night, when they were entertaining the troops, they summoned them. The next day, eight men showed up with stolen blankets from the barracks. Sometimes, it might be okay to steal. They came bearing wood, tools, and supplies to insulate the two rooms from the cold. The orphanage kept growing as the ladies continued to summon the servicemen to come help. Rooms were added on like you would see in the crazy house at Disneyland. Wherever they could get space, they added on. This orphanage is still running today.

When Sara and Yvonne came back to California, Governor Ronald Reagan heard about what they had done and called a meeting with them. Nancy Reagan told them there was also a problem of abuse in America and personally gave them their first $5,000 check to start an organization to help abused and abandoned children here in the United States. Many years later, Sara and Yvonne are still tirelessly helping children through the largest child protection charity in the country. Over 12 million children have been saved from child abuse through Childhelp. They have 24-hour hotlines, child advocacy centers, highly trained counselors, foster home training centers, homes, and entire villages for the worst abuse cases in the country. As a result, they have been nominated eight times for the Nobel Peace Prize.

My favorite part of Childhelp is that it is a Christian organization. Sara and Yvonne's philosophy is to introduce these children to a loving Father, *the* loving Father. They have chapels on each of their campuses and a full-time pastor to teach the children that even though people may have failed them, God will never fail them. The stories of redemption from these children are astounding. I went to Phoenix, where Childhelp is headquartered, to help them set up a new advocacy center. They set up these centers in buildings with the police department, legal teams, and therapists. Childhelp takes over half the building and converts it into the happiest-looking place in the world. It's like walking into Disneyland. When the children come in traumatized, they at least have a place to feel safe and loved. This is just one of the many ministries they do in Childhelp. When I arrived, ready to help set up one of the new buildings, I had no idea what I was getting myself into. Let's just say I was outdone by two women in their 80s. We worked from 7:00 in the morning until sometimes midnight, getting the rooms all set up for the children. This particular building was transformed from office spaces to 12 bedrooms, baby rooms for infants, game rooms, playrooms for the younger children, kitchens, dining rooms, offices for the counselors, and a chapel. We started with nothing and only had a week to get it all done.

Sara and Yvonne aren't just Christians. They live out their faith. They put the footwork into their faith. God has kept this charity and ministry going when businessmen would tell them, "This won't work. The need is too great, and the programs are too expensive." Many years later, they are like the "little engines that could," they keep going and will not stop until the Lord takes them home. One thing that astonished me was how Sara and Yvonne heard from the Lord.

One night, we were at dinner, and I asked them, "How do you hear so clearly from the Lord? What is your secret?" Their answer was so simple, yet so profound. They said, "We listen." It was a true epiphany to me. Right then, I realized when I spoke to God, it was a one-way conversation. After listing everything I needed, I never took the time to listen.

Sara said they pray every day but devote much of their prayer time to just listening for what the Lord wants them to do, where to go, and who to meet. There was a time in their organization, around the crash of the economy in 2008, when many people stopped giving.

Most of the individuals advising them said, "It's time to close shop on some of the programs. The villages are too expensive to keep running. They require too many staff members, as the children who are coming are the worst cases and sometimes need one-on-one help." The Childhelp villages receive the children who have been passed around from foster care homes and delinquent homes. Sometimes, they've been in 20 different places before they were 18 years old. The government system has given up on them. Many times, Childhelp is the last hope. One boy came into their village and couldn't look anyone in the eye. His father had burned his entire face with an iron, causing severe scarring. He grew his hair out long to completely cover his face. When Yvonne and Sara returned to the facility for their annual Christmas party for the children, they were overjoyed. That young man was up on stage, front and center, singing Christmas carols to Jesus as he starred in the Christmas play. His hair was cut, revealing a face filled with joy, not shame. He learned that Jesus loves him no matter what.

These women knew that if God gave them the responsibility of taking care of the children, He would provide for them. So, they dug their heels in and prayed. During one of the toughest years, at the eleventh hour, a woman who previously had never heard about their charity, had never met Sara or Yvonne, or ever saw their facilities sent a million-dollar check that arrived the day payroll was due. These women refused to close shop, knowing the Lord had told them He would take care of everything. They heard Him when everyone told them it was impossible.

While I was there helping set up the new advocacy center, I asked Sara and Yvonne if I could pick up McDonald's Happy Meals for the children. I called the facility, and they said 17 children were coming in to spend the night. When I arrived at the facility, I had a huge lump in my throat, fighting back tears as I handed out the Happy Meals.

There was the most beautiful, angel-faced little Hispanic boy. He was probably four years old. He was so traumatized, not knowing where he was or why he was there. He was taken away from a home of abuse, which was all he knew. So, he didn't understand why he was taken away. He wouldn't touch his dinner and stared straight ahead. By then, it was 7:00 p.m., much past the time when the other children had finished eating. I knelt beside him and asked, "Are you not hungry?" No response. Then I asked him, "Would you like me to unwrap your meal for you?" Again, no response. I unwrapped his meal and laid it out in front of him. He wouldn't touch it. I knew he had to be starving. Who knows when his last meal was? I didn't know what to do, so I prayed and asked the Lord to help me reach this beautiful child. That's when I heard from the Lord. I moved closer to the little boy and whispered in his ear, "May I tell you a secret?" Still no response. "Here is the secret…" I began singing an old Sunday school song I had sung as a child. "Jesus loves you, this I know, for the Bible tells me so. Little ones to Him belong. They are weak, but He is strong. Yes, Jesus loves you. Yes, Jesus loves you. Yes, Jesus loves you. The Bible tells me so."

Halfway through the song, he grabbed his burger and crawled into my lap. The hand with his burger in it wrapped around my neck entwined. He put his head on my shoulder and began eating. Very rarely can I get through that story without crying. I stayed as long as they let me that night. He held my hand and came with me everywhere. All that precious little boy needed to hear was that someone loved him. I believe children have an innate sense that their Creator, Jesus, loves them. We are created to know Jesus loves us and to have a relationship with Him. That little boy knew I was telling him the truth the minute I began singing to him. They had to peel me away from that child when it was bedtime. I have wondered and prayed for years for that little boy. If I weren't single or going through menopause, I would've taken that child to raise. The system isn't allowed to tell me where he is now, but I know Jesus has him.

Shortly after being in Phoenix to set up that center, the second incident happened which taught me further how to hear from the Lord. When the Lord gave me that condo in Dallas, I figured it was a haven and an escape. Maybe that was one reason. But there would be more. My friend Bill told me about a small church that started with a group of people who came together and just prayed. It wasn't meant to be a traditional church but rather a safe place for all to come and pray and seek God anytime they wanted. It was called Upperroom and situated on top of a veterinary clinic. When the worship started, the animals downstairs joined in. By the time I heard about Upperroom, it had already become a church, and people started coming from all over Dallas, thrilled to find a place to worship freely. The first time I walked in the door, I knew I was "home."

Upperroom has worship and prayer for two hours almost every morning, noon, and evening. It attracts people of all kinds and never passes judgment. In fact, I've been to church services with men in full drag. They feel safe and loved – and are.

I am absolutely amazed at these young people's dedication and enthusiasm in their commitment to serving the Lord. I see all these "hipsters," some from very staunch religious backgrounds, some tattooed out, and some with dreadlocks. Then there are former soccer stars and models, people coming out of sexual addictions—and that's just the staff! I cry every service seeing these young people from all walks of life, watching God change their lives, give them purpose, and totally commit to serving Jesus. Thankfully, we never have to "qualify" to serve Jesus. I love the saying, "You gotta catch a fish before you can clean it." It's Jesus who does the cleaning.

I began going to the worship and prayer set at 6:00 a.m. A worship team comes and spearheads the worship music, yet all of us are open to whatever the Holy Spirit has for us that morning. Some people get up with a scripture they feel compelled to read. Sometimes, we all get in a circle and pray for our nation and leaders. You name it, we go for it. At first, this was challenging for me. Not being with the group but teaching my mind to concentrate and meditate on the Lord for two hours. It was like herding cats for me. I would go to the prayer set, and within a few minutes I would be in my own head deciding what furniture pieces went on what walls in a new property I was renovating. Or what I was going to have for lunch and even which emails I needed to answer. I was an attention-deficit disaster. I would go so far as to count the calories I had the day before and then be mad at myself for eating so much. I was there physically but not mentally or spiritually.

I realized our minds are like muscles. We must train them and get them under submission, just as we must go to a gym to train our muscles.

When I was in my 40s, I remember reaching up for a glass in an upper cabinet when Armie came from behind me and started flapping that skin all older women get under their arms. They were flapping with the breeze as he swung them back and forth, singing, "Now let me tell you the story 'bout a man named Jed…"

If you really want the truth, ask a child! I knew right then it wasn't going to get any better unless I got my butt to the gym and did something about it. And my mind wasn't going to get any better about concentrating and devoting that time with the Lord if I didn't put an effort into this. So, I kept showing up, daydreaming, but showing up. One of the first things I did to improve was to put my phone away. I used to take it to look up Bible verses, only to check texts and see who I needed to email back. After months of showing up, the time would fly by as I worshiped the Lord. The best part is that I started hearing from the Lord. That subtle, sweet voice of the Lord would begin giving me ideas. For instance, writing this book kept gnawing at me in those prayer sets. It was something I had put off for years. I finally said, "Okay, Lord, but I'm embarrassed to even tell anyone I'm writing a book. I'm not interesting enough and certainly not a literary giant. And yet, if just one person is touched and comes to know You and learns to forgive as I did, then I'll do it."

Even today, as my children are grown and I've been given the gift of time, I'm going to keep showing up and see how God moves in my life. This goes for all of us. It's about how the Lord equips us for what He calls us to do. I heard a pastor say, "God isn't interested in our ability. He's interested in our availability."

My whole life I'd been reaching for His hands, provisions in tow. After connecting with Childhelp and Upperroom, I learned to reach out to His heart and seek His will for my life. It's no longer about what I want Him to do with my list of wants. I'm learning to tap into His will by learning to hear and listen. My prayers and conversations with God are no longer one-sided. And our talks have become so much better.

Let's pray together

God, if I ever feel distant from You, it s just me who has moved. You are a loving and consistent God, just waiting for us to turn everything over to You so You can move on our behalf. Help me draw closer to You every single day of my life. I love you, not because of what You do for me but for who You are. Amen

Chapter 17

The Gifts of Our Father

Elijah was a mighty prophet of the Lord during the days of King Ahab and his evil wife, Queen Jezebel. She vowed to have every prophet of the Lord murdered. Good luck with that! All her false prophets of Baal were destroyed instead. Her demise was falling out of a window and being splattered on the stone ground with dogs eating her flesh, just as Elijah prophesied. If that story doesn't encourage us to "hurt not God's anointed," nothing will. Mighty miracles of God were done through Elijah. He had a trusted, Godly helper, Elisha, who forsook everything to minister alongside him. When Elijah was about to be taken up to heaven, he wanted to bless Elisha for being such a faithful friend and help in the mission God had called him into. "When they had crossed over, Elijah said to Elisha, 'Ask what I shall do for you before I am taken from you.' And Elisha said, 'Please, let a double portion of your spirit be upon me.'" (2 Kings 2:9, NKJV)

Since my divorce, my mother had a severe stroke that affected her physically. A few years later, my father had a stroke, which affected him more mentally. There had been some rough years in our family. My parents had to give up traveling all over the world with their healing ministry. My son, Viktor, went to Oral Roberts University for his first two years of college in Tulsa. What a joy that was for my parents as they had never had grandchildren in their town. Viktor is the most relational son you could ever dream of having. He and his dad spoke at least once a day and many times twice a day. He was his father's stability. I also speak with him almost daily. That's such a great joy in my life. Viktor would go see my parents in Tulsa several times a week while in school and always brought friends over to their house on the weekends. My mom would cook for them and make them snickerdoodle cookies. I'm grateful that Viktor gleaned from my parent's faithfulness. It's a reminder of how "the blessings of a generation are passed down." I always wanted to glean from them as well. After my divorce was finalized, I made a special trip to Tulsa and asked my dad to pray over me, as I wanted that same double portion Elisha asked for from Elijah.

I asked dad to pray for a double portion of his healing gift and business acumen. He is not only a wise businessman who sought the Lord, but he is also extremely disciplined and crosses every "t" and dots every "i".

Michael used to call my methods of business "organized chaos." I could renovate a 15,000-square-foot home down to the studs and have the notes, floor plans, electrical plans, lists of materials, and more written down on a napkin from the restaurant the night before. I had every single design detail in my head, down to where every electrical outlet should be placed. Yet you would look at my desk, and it looked like the office in *The Absent-Minded Professor*. For some reason, it just worked for me. I am more of the creative side of the brain, but I also wanted the business side. That's why I went to Tulsa, asking for my dad's wisdom and organization. I have accidentally forgotten a lunch or two, leaving friends waiting. I've lost checks and forgotten appointments. Well, you get the picture. I figured I didn't have that gift of organization because I had not asked for it or was not disciplined enough. When my dad prayed for me, I was kind of hoping and envisioning a lightning bolt moment when I would really feel the presence of God, confirming it was done. I felt nothing. Then, my dad reminded me how, as believers, we go by faith, not by how or what we feel. So, I left Tulsa and returned to my normal life.

A few weeks later, I planned a trip to New York to see Kathie Lee. She never missed a day praying for me during the end of my marriage and trudging my way through the painful divorce. Neither did her daughter, Cassidy. Faithful friends. We can go without seeing each other for months. Then, when we get together, it's like we had lunch together the day before. When we do have lunch, we can stretch it out for many hours.

I would ride into New York City with Kathie Lee, hang out with her while she taped her show, and then have a fabulous marathon lunch before heading back to her home in Greenwich. It's one of my favorite things in the world to do. I woke up the third day I was there in Greenwich and had this inkling that I needed to just stay there and spend some time with the Lord. I put my iPod on, loaded with praise and worship music, paired with sermons from amazing ministers from around the country, and took off for a long prayer walk.

As I walked and walked, I saw an older woman crossing a busy street. She was literally dragging one of her legs behind her. I could tell she had no function in that leg. By the time she got to the other side of the street, she was so exhausted that she sat on the bus stop bench. As I walked past her, the thought came to my mind, which I believe was from the Lord, "You asked for this gift. Now go back and pray for her."

But I began arguing with the Lord in my carnal mind, saying, "God, it's a busy street. I'll look like a weirdo. What if she doesn't believe in miracles like I do? And by the way, can we start with a cold? I mean, a dead leg?!"

Then this thought came to my mind, "You can't heal a cold or a dead leg. This has nothing to do with you. Go back and pray for her."

I turned around, walked back, and asked the woman, "May I ask you a question? Do you believe in Jesus?" She said, "Yes, I do." I bravely proceeded, "What has happened to your leg?" She explained that she was in a bad car accident, and it destroyed all the nerves from her back going down into that leg. The doctors told her the nerve damage was irreparable and she would never be able to walk again normally on that leg.

"Do you believe Jesus can heal you?" I loved her honest response. She said, "I don't know."

"Well, ma'am, I do. Jesus loves you so much. He wants you healed. Are you open to me kneeling right here on this busy street and asking Jesus to heal your leg?" "Yes," she said. I knelt right there and said a simple prayer, asking Jesus to heal her nerves and leg. He had already reminded me that this had nothing to do with me. I knew this as I had seen my dad pray for tens of thousands of people to be healed. But why was it harder for me to believe He could do it through me? My mind always seems to get in the way. The crazy thing is I have prayed for people my entire life to be healed, but this time, I was asking for that double portion. I had to step up my faith and expect the miracle immediately for this woman, just like I had seen with my dad.

Next thing I knew, the woman got up and began walking completely normal on both legs. I praised God the entire walk home and kept thinking, "God, I know You could have sent anyone to pray for that woman's healing, but thank you for giving me the privilege of seeing this woman restored, not only physically but spiritually. I can only imagine the new faith this woman discovered through her miraculous healing."

In reading the four gospels in the New Testament, thousands of people came to know Christ when they saw and experienced miraculous healings that Jesus performed and how He commissioned His followers to go out and do the same thing. Jesus said, "They will be able to lay hands on the sick, and they will be healed." (Mark 16:18)

The next supernatural healing I personally experienced was when I was going through security at the airport. I saw a couple in front of me. The wife was in a wheelchair, so ill that she couldn't hold her head up. Her coloring did not look good at all, either. Again, I felt like the Lord wanted me to pray for them. This time I said, "Oh, Lord, it's jam-packed here. I can't stop the line of people trying to get through security. I'll get through security and then pray for them at their gate."

I got through security after them and lost track of them. Wouldn't you know I went around all the gates trying to find them? I was rationalizing with God about the crowds instead of just stepping up to the plate. I went around three times and couldn't find them. All the while, I apologized to the Lord for not doing it when He asked me. Feeling defeated, I went into the American Airlines lounge. BAM! They were in a quiet corner where I could speak with them. I walked over to them and told them how I felt like I had missed the chance from the Lord to see them before their flights. I asked if I could pray for them. The couple began to cry and said they were on their way back from Israel and had to leave early because the wife had become so ill. They didn't know what was wrong with her. She couldn't even raise her arms. Just like with the woman on the street, I knelt and asked Jesus to heal her body. He knows what is wrong, and I knew He could heal her from the top of her head to the bottom of her feet. We hugged and cried together. Then, I walked into the bathroom. The next thing I knew, the woman walked in right behind me. Jesus had healed her! We rejoiced and thanked the Lord together.

Now for the humbling part. I do miss, and I miss big time from the Lord. I even asked Todd White, who has an amazing healing ministry, and asked him, "Do you ever miss from the Lord? Do you pray for people to be healed, and they aren't healed?" Todd told me that when he first felt called into ministry to pray for people to be healed, he prayed for over 200 people before he saw his first miraculous healing. That didn't mean the people were not healed, but it may have been a gradual healing that he would never see. However, Todd kept doing what he felt called to do, and his faith remained strong. I think the Lord sees if we are relentless and if we will keep showing up. After 200, Todd kept praying for people to be healed in spite of not seeing instant miracles. He knew Jesus healed, so he kept on.

Then, one day, he prayed for a man who had walked out of a wheelchair at Walmart. Nowadays, Todd is completely out of control! That's a good thing. He prays for every person he encounters, including my favorite barista, Jay, in a Beverly Hills Starbucks. One day, after our group got our coffees and walked out of the store, Todd told us he needed to go back and pray for Jay.

"Jay, you have a bad knee, and Jesus wants to heal you," Todd said.

Todd also has the gift of knowledge, seeing people's needs before they even tell him. If that doesn't build faith before praying, nothing will.

It turned out, Jay did have a bad knee! But there was no way Todd could have known unless the Holy Spirit had revealed that to him. Our group prayed over Jay, and Jesus healed his knee immediately. Jay started crying and moving that knee. I'm sure everyone in Starbucks thought we were crazy, but all the mocking in the world is worth that one healing. We walked away with our lattes and so much more.

In thinking of the misses, one day, I felt like I was supposed to go up and pray for a particular young man in the gym. I asked him if he had any ailments he needed a prayer for because Jesus would like to heal him.

He was about 6'8. He looked down at me and said, "No, not at all."

I felt like a smashed bug. Then, other times when I prayed, it seemed nothing had happened. Again, Jesus is faithful. We don't know how the Lord is dealing with a person's heart. That healing may come, but that doesn't mean we'll see it. I have decided I would rather err on the side of taking that opportunity. I may feel like an idiot at times, but at least I know I have shown up. It's all about restoration, and that is something I have found success and fulfillment in.

Let's pray together

So many times in the Bible, Lord, You said to people who came to You for healing,   Your faith has made you well." The Bible also teaches us about the   gift of faith." Jesus, there is no distance in prayer, and I pray You give me and everyone reading this the   gift of faith" to believe nothing is impossible with You. Amen

Chapter 18

Sons: A Love Letter

How in the world can two human beings, born from the same mom and dad, who came out of the same birth canal, be from different universes?

It would be impossible to write a book without including my two favorite people in the world–my sons, Armie and Viktor. They already know how much I love them, but I also want the world to know. Despite all our failures as human beings, I love my sons in the most unconditional way possible on this Earth.

Since our family has been dragged through the mud, especially in the last few years, I must address the "elephant" in the room, much to my chagrin. Otherwise, *Hammered* isn't a complete or honest depiction of why I wanted to write this book in the first place.

It's one thing to have family dirt, which no family is unscathed from, but it's an entirely different thing when it's spread all over the national papers, magazines, trades, documentaries, and trending on social media, especially when there are just sprinkles of truth amongst many untruths. Dirt sells; sweet, endearing stories mostly don't. I'm not writing to defend my family, but I also can't sweep it under the rug. No one knows us Hammers more than I do. I had the privilege of spending 25 years with Michael, more time with the patriarch Armand than most in the family, and I spent time with Michael's father, Julian. His wonderful mother, Sue, was one of my best friends. And, of course, certainly no one knows Armie and Viktor Hammer more than their mama.

I knew them before I laid eyes on them. Three weeks before my due date with Armie, I woke up and knew the Lord told me today was the day he was coming into this world. So, I got up and went to town for a mani/pedi. Yes, that's true. At that moment, I thought, "You can't have your legs in a stirrup without your toes looking good!" I also washed my hair, shaved, and packed my bags.

I called Michael at the office and said to meet me in Westwood for a triple espresso to get this party started. I drank diet cokes and coffee throughout my entire pregnancy. We didn't know any better. Thankfully, it didn't seem to hurt. I called my doctor and told him I was having my baby today. "Well, are you having any contractions?" I replied, "No, not yet, but I'm coming in." I'm sure Dr. Monoson thought I was mad. I'm sure Michael thought the same. Sure enough, I started feeling contractions by the time I got to the coffee shop. When we arrived at UCLA, I was dilated to seven, and within five hours, our gift came into the world. I decided to do natural childbirth. Looking back, I wonder, what the flip was I thinking?!

When I gave birth to Armie, his great-grandfather, Armand, was 87 years old and still traveling the world running Occidental Petroleum. He was in Russia when Armie was born. I got a telegram (remember those?) that said, "Dru and Michael, I couldn't be more thrilled about my new great-grandson. It would mean the world to me if you would name him Armand." Wait, what?

Did I read that correctly? He wanted me to name my tiny, 5lb, 8oz baby Armand? Furthermore, Armand Hammer was a well-known name in America at that time. That's a lot for a child to carry. Then again, Armand was so good to me. Couldn't I grant his request? Though he was a smaller-in-stature man, 5'5", he carried a lot of power. My mama didn't raise no fools. Armand, it would be! It was my sister, Lisa, who came up with calling him "Armie." Now that was appealing. When Armie became an actor, people thought Armie Hammer was a stage name because it was so unique. But, seriously, how would you just make up a name like that?

With a name intact and a clean bill of health, we brought Armie home. He was purple, long, skinny, and had a full head of coal-black hair that spiked like a monkey. Soon, Armie's black hair fell out, and this magnificent thick head of white and blonde came in. Who knew when he started so puny that he would grow into a 6'5" giant with a size 15 shoe and enormous hands. He was always average height until one year he grew eight inches. People talk about growing pains, but he physically had them. He would walk up a flight of stairs, and since his growth plates were so far apart, his hip would give out on him, and he would go tumbling down the stairs.

When Michael and I brought Armie home, we spent hours a day just staring at him. There is no deeper love in the world than bringing a child into this world. That child was so beautiful and crazy talented. Whatever he picked up, he was good at. Give him a yoyo, and he will spin that thing around in circles and do all these captivating tricks. He wanted to play the guitar. Would you know that in a few years, he was playing completely by ear? If he heard it on the radio, he could play it. He was the entertainment for our family.

I call Armie my "payback kid" because he was just like me as a child. He didn't want to sleep or waste time, so he was up every morning at 5:00. It didn't matter when he went to bed. He was ornery, just like I was, but he had the kindest heart and always thought the best of people. And boy, was he funny. Still is. Not surprising since his father was one of the funniest people. Armie has that same hilarious sense of humor. He also has a brilliant mind and photographic memory.

Many years later, when I visited the set of *The Lone Ranger*, there must have been over 400 people working. Armie knew every person's name. He walked up to everyone and spoke with them, even knowing their children's names. To a mama, that is better than your son being the Lone Ranger. I was proud of how he treated everyone with the respect they all deserved. If you sit down and watch the show *Jeopardy* with Armie, he knows every answer and crazy weird facts. Once, the answer was "The science of determining a tree's age by looking at its growth rings." The question was, "What is dendrochronology?" Armie knew that! I remember that so clearly because I thought it was a rerun, and Armie had already seen it. His friends, Ashton and Tyler, were there and said, "No, this was a new episode, and he does this every time." Both of my sons are voracious readers, and the crazy part is that they remember everything they read.

###

The week before my due date with Viktor, once again, I knew I was having my baby that day. I called Dr. Monoson with the news that I was coming in to have my baby. I did not have a contraction in sight.

"Dru, a woman can guess and get it right one time, but no woman knows the exact date every time," he responded logically.

I confidently replied, "You're right, but God knows, so I'm coming in, but first, I'm headed to get a mani/pedi!"

Sure enough, Michael met me for espressos, and by the time we got to the hospital, I was dilated to nine centimeters. I had Viktor in less than two hours. Dr. Monoson couldn't believe it. He said I could have had that baby on the sidewalk. Well, wouldn't that have been a pretty sight!

Viktor came out of the womb and didn't make a peep. He was the easiest child I could ever raise. I truly don't remember ever having to discipline him. He was a child of few words.

I remember driving the boys to school one day, and I asked them what their favorite Bible verse was. Viktor said, "Let the words of the wise be few." That pretty much sums up Viktor. He has always been the sweetest and quirkiest person. He also has a funny and quick sense of humor.

Throughout school, he gravitated to the underdogs. His "Aunt" Candace came over one day and saw Viktor playing with all his friends and said, "What is this, the United Nations?"

Viktor was so attached to me and Luz. I carried him for the first five years of his life. If he were in my arms, he would be happy. He hated school. He didn't want to be away from us and his comfort zone. My sister, Mel, and I took him to his first day of preschool, and he freaked out. He was sobbing. He just didn't want to leave me. It broke my heart, but the teacher said, "Don't worry. He will adjust and be fine and have a wonderful time with the other children."

When I left, he was face-down, bawling on this miniature couch. When Mel and I returned to pick him up three hours later, he had not left the couch and was heaving in tears. Having to take him back for day two was excruciating.

I'm not sure he ever wanted to go to school that entire year. He refused to get dressed every morning. We had to force him to put clothes on. He would complain about his stomach hurting every morning. I always thought that was the way for him to be able to stay home from school.

Come to find out, he was lactose intolerant. That was a failure on my part. I felt horrible. Oh, I loved that child and was so sad the day he didn't want me to carry him anymore.

The day he went to college, I went with him to get him all settled in his dorm room. As he was walking me out to the rental car to say goodbye, he handed me the house keys from home and said, "Oh, I won't need these. You can take them home for me."

Suddenly, the tables turned, and I felt like he was on that first day of school. I started bawling right there in the parking lot and threw my arms around this big 6'3" grown son of mine.

He subtly said to me, "Mom, you might want to get going so you don't miss your flight." In other words, "You are embarrassing me. You are such a hot mess, please go." What happened to my child who never wanted to leave my sight?

When Viktor was born, Armand was in town and came up to the hospital. He was so thrilled to have a second great-grandson. When he was holding our new baby, he said to me, "Dru, as you know, my brother Victor has always been my best friend. It would mean the world to me if you would name him Viktor." With Michael being the only grandson, having another Armand and Viktor was very important.

Uhhhhh, we weren't thinking of that name, much like we weren't thinking of the name Armand. It's hard to call a baby such a grown-up name. However, once again, since Armand was so good to us, we were happy to oblige. For nine years, we called Viktor "Happy." It just fit since he never cried. "Happy" came home from school in the 5th grade and said he was not going to be called "Happy" anymore because kids teased him in school, saying his brothers were Dopey and Sneezy from the Snow White dwarfs. As easy as Viktor was when things were important to him, and he made his mind up, there was no changing it.

Now Armie wasn't so mellow. We called him "Armando El Destructo". He would crash his remote-controlled cars. When he and Viktor started riding motorcycles, we had to build mounds for them to jump. That's why he could do all his stunts in *The Lone Ranger* and *Man from U.N.C.L.E.* The best way I can describe Armie as a kid was "Curious George," like the character who got into everything. That can be a recipe for disaster when this childhood was surrounded by construction sites and construction tools from all the properties I renovated.

One afternoon, I went outside to my brand-new car and noticed there were all these funny spots on the back of it. As I got closer, I saw mud dots all over my car. Well, Armie was about five years old, and he was out watching all the contractors hammering, drilling, and sawing. When the contractors took a lunch break, he got the drill and drilled about eight holes in the back of my car. Soon, he had the lightbulb moment, and maybe he shouldn't have done that, so he made mud and filled the holes. He didn't get in trouble for doing that. I mean, no one would have thought to tell him he shouldn't do that. But he did get in trouble for trying to cover it up and lying about it.

I know you're thinking, "You let your young sons play with electric drills?" Looking back, I do wonder what I was thinking, but I was a laid-back mom. My sons had the run of the house. I never had a living room where children couldn't go in because of breakable things or expensive furniture. The amazing thing was nothing was ever damaged or broken. Maybe because they weren't told not to go in there like it was the forbidden fruit. Those rooms were just not as appealing as the rooms with all the toys.

With years of construction going on during their childhood, I renovated 27 properties in 25 years. It seemed our home was always a construction site. I tried to make it fun for the boys. Viktor always built a "box city" when we moved. He would take all the boxes and rolls and rolls of duct tape and build tunnels and rooms with all the boxes. Our entire backyard, hallways throughout the house and rooms would be filled with a "box city."

I never knew where they were around the house. That would last for weeks and maybe even months in the backyard until it rained then our entire yard was filled with soggy boxes. The "box city" was in ruins.

For some of their birthday parties I would have the same food truck come to our house that was there every day for our construction workers. The food truck would park in our yard next to the pool and the kids had free rein of that food truck.

They would walk away with handfuls of candy bars, hotdogs, hamburgers, and sodas. Every dietician's greatest nightmare! It's amazing that the moms spoke to me again, as I could only imagine the sugar highs I sent their children home with. But the best birthday party Viktor had was taking a group of friends to Legoland. It was his mecca seeing cities built out of Legos.

Viktor also wore a Superman cape for years. My sister, Lisa, was visiting, and sure enough, Viktor came out wearing a towel safety-pinned around his neck as a cape. For his birthday, she sewed him (she was one of those super moms) a Superman cape with the logo sewn on it. He wore it every day from when he was two years old until he was five years old.

He believed he was Superman and would jump off of everything. At three years old, he jumped off the back of the couch and limped around for a few days. Come to find out, my Superman broke his foot. Yet another sign that I may be too laid back. I never rushed my kids to the doctor. He had this tiny, four-inch cast, and it was so spankin 'cute. I got a kick out of it. The cast didn't slow him down in the least. He would run around in the cast with his Superman cape and underwear. The funniest part was that his tiny body was built like a superhero. It was unreal. He had a little tiny butt and this wide barrel chest and an actual six-pack. He was like a miniature, ripped bodybuilder. I'm biased, but he was the cutest child alive.

Viktor and his father had a building and mechanical bug in common. They would take motorcycles apart, have the tanks and fenders custom painted and then put them back together. Michael and Viktor even built a miniature motorcycle together and had the Superman logo with flames coming from it painted on the gas tank. It was like déjà vu. I guess my little boy who wore a Superman cape never grew out of that fascination. Magic Johnson saw that motorcycle at a show and wanted to buy it, but Viktor wasn't ready to part with it.

Michael bonded with the boys with his love of cars. He would take the boys to car shows and he even took them when they each turned 16 years old to Carmel to race car driving school. I wasn't sure that was a very good idea to teach them how to speed but neither of my sons have been in a car accident or have been given a ticket. Maybe it's because they learned defensive driving in those race car driving schools. Plus, my years of prayers of protection.

To this day, my boys give me grief because they had this thick head of blonde hair, and I cut their hair in a bowl cut. The problem is, I cut it myself, so they have many school pictures where their hair is just a little eschewed. To make it worse, I dressed them alike. When we would go to church or travel, I put them in little navy-blue blazers with the Polo emblem, white button-down shirts, pleated khaki pants, and saddle oxfords until they graduated to penny loafers and then driving shoes. They looked like they walked out of a preppy handbook.

We moved to the Cayman Islands when the boys were five and seven. I loved it when they got to the age where we could play together. I knew I was a boy mom and prayed for two boys. In the Cayman Islands, we lived in a private gated community. The development was new. Only one full-time family was living there. They had a seven-year-old son, John. The three boys were inseparable. They all had dirt bikes, and they took over the entire development. They built mounds of dirt so they could jump their bikes. They had golf carts that Michael souped up that went 30 miles per hour. Nothing like putting small children behind a golf cart that went that fast! Viktor fell off (or pushed; that is still a debate that goes on) and broke his two front teeth off. Perhaps the golf carts weren't such a good idea after all, but they certainly had a blast in them, not to mention they became tremendous drivers with real cars.

Then let's give them all machetes. They would go around climbing coconut trees and cutting down coconuts. With all the original landscaping it seemed like a jungle at their size. They would be gone for hours cutting down the "jungle." It was pretty much a Swiss Family Robinson adventure for our sons.

Viktor was our true animal lover and found stray cats he took in and called them Luz and Lena, after our housekeepers we missed and loved so much in the States. We couldn't get them papers for the Caymans, which was the saddest part of moving. To this day, the boys say that living in the Cayman Islands was the happiest years of their lives.

No one ever had to entertain Viktor. He would build things, take things apart, and always figure out how and why they worked. All he ever wanted for birthdays and Christmas gifts were Legos. He built elaborate, very difficult Lego sets that were advanced for his years.

We would have to make him stop to come down for dinner. To this day, I'm so amazed by how intricate Legos are. When I'm buying some for my grandson, I send an architectural one to Viktor. Angie, Viktor's wife, will call and say, "Thanks a lot. Viktor hasn't left the house all weekend building that Lego set!" Still a kid at heart.

Viktor is so hyper-focused on things that he is a bulldog until he accomplishes his goal. His determination has always been there, but I totally credit Angie for buttoning him down in school. He was never a great student until he met Angie in college.

Michael and I were going through our terrible divorce during the year they met, and Viktor was so depressed. Angie told him if he wanted to date her, he could date her in the library, as she graduated magna cum laude. He immediately straightened up and graduated with top grades, which got him on his path. I will always be indebted to Angie for those times when he was feeling so lost during our divorce.

Viktor was working for his dad at the time of our divorce. He had a front-row seat to witness the lifestyle patterns of his father's changing, alcohol and drug abuse, which is something none of us had ever seen when we were a family.

I am so proud of Viktor. He worked hard to get a job with Morgan Stanley. He went through months of interviews, aptitude tests, and regulation certifications. When he first took the job, they shipped him off to New York City for training.

I was on my knees praying for him, not because I didn't think he could do it, but because New York City is out of any young man's box feeling out his new career. He was always a shy child and was always the son who was happy to be in the background. Now, he was being pushed into the big city, making calls and taking meetings with established business people he had never met before. Amazingly, he soared and loved it.

Being stretched showed him his capability even though it was initially out of his comfort zone. Now, he will talk your ears off about the stock market and business and has no qualms about reaching out to foundations and ministries to help invest for them. He called me one day and said it didn't inspire him to help make wealthy people wealthier. He wanted to help charitable organizations and ministries invest their funds and help them have more money to give away to help others. You know that was a happy day in my life.

I learned from my parents. When my sons became young adults, it was a gift to see that generational blessing being passed down to another generation. That's when I feel like I have done my job as a parent. Even amongst my many failures, God overcompensates, and I have had the privilege of watching my sons treat people with such kindness and do wonderful things for others.

God sees and blesses us back. Less than 11 percent make it past the first year at his financial firm. Now, Viktor is already one of the vice presidents of his division and has been selected to join a group in his company that is one of the largest accounts for 501c3 organizations helping grow charities and ministries. He needed to get his MBA before moving forward with this group he joined. Not only did he get his degree, but he also finished it early in the semester, working full-time and taking his courses at night.

Angie was working on her masters, too. She is now working on her doctorate. They are perfectly matched for each other. They love to study, learn, and live private lives.

Now Armie chose a very different path. When he was 10 years old, he told us he was going to be an actor. Since we were living in the Cayman Islands, I couldn't figure out where that came from. Now, I know it was God's plan. Always the encouraging mom, I said, "Armie, that is a terrible career! There's so much rejection, and few make it. And the lifestyles seem so self-absorbed, and many seem to have such dark lives."

While that wasn't my most inspiring pep talk, but I was speaking from experience. I had lived in Los Angeles, and I saw it first-hand. Few child actors can transform into adult actors, so they lose their childhood being on set. Then it is all about them, especially if they are churning out the money for the production companies. When they grow up, they can be discarded, and it can ruin their self-esteem and even their lives. I didn't want that for my son. We moved back to Los Angeles when the boys were going into middle school. Since Armie was persistent, I took him to a few acting classes. I saw all these stage moms living vicariously through their kids. I just wanted Armie to have a normal childhood; little did I know.

Michael and I agreed that when he was older, he could drive himself to acting classes and auditions if he still wanted to act. Then we would support his decision… maybe.

Armie never liked school. He was bullied terribly when we moved back to LA. He was the new kid on the block in a private Christian school in the Palisades. However, he was popular with the girls, and the boys hated him for it.

When your child cries himself to sleep because he is being bullied, there is no deeper pain for parents. I advised him to "turn the other cheek and be kind to the bullies." Once again, practical advice, but not helpful. The bullying got worse. After many trips to the principal's office to tell the administration what was happening, nothing was done. Michael sat Armie down for a game plan. He said, "Being nice doesn't work with

151

boys. Sometimes, you need to stake your claim and retaliate." That week, when the bullying started up again, Armie punched one bully in the face, breaking his nose, and threw another bully in the dumpster. It seemed to stop, or at least subside. I didn't advise fighting, but you gotta do what you gotta do.

It reminds me of a saying I love: "Tough times don't last, but tough people do."

I always say, "hurt people end up hurting people if they have not found the love of God." It's a vicious cycle, and these hardships can cause us to either continue that pattern or choose to have sympathy and empathy to help others because they understand the deep hurt. Platforms are given in life to make a difference and help others through our own suffering.

Like Candace Lightner, who lost her daughter, Cari, at age 13 years old to a drunk driver. She had to endure the worst pain any mother could ever go through.

Yet, she chose to make a difference through her hardship and started MADD [Mothers Against Drunk Driving] in 1980. She has single-handedly changed drinking and driving laws in the country. With that, I'm sure she's saved millions of lives.

When we give our hardships to God, no suffering goes in vain. One of my proudest moments with Armie was when he booked his first big commercial movie. There was a red carpet premiere at the Chinese Mann Theater in Hollywood.

As Armie was walking down the red carpet, who was standing at the entrance door of the theater with the employer's uniform on collecting the tickets? It was the very young man who was the biggest perpetrator of Armie's bullying in middle school.

I watched Armie go up and give him a big hug and ask how he was doing and how good it was to see him. Watching my son receive accolades on the red carpet was a proud moment for me as his mother.

But seeing him give love to his former enemy was like my cup runneth over.

Armie got his first starring role after years and years of toiling, acting classes, coaching, and beating the pavement amongst years of rejection. Yes, he may have had it easier than some, but it doesn't take away from the hard work he put into his plan A.

He knew even through all the rejections, there was no plan B for him. We had him take college courses through the first two years before it was obvious that acting was what he would do full-time.

In his mind, college was a waste of time. Michael and I prayed about it, and we decided to support him for the first four years as if he were in college, then he is on his own. Years later, the press put articles out that we had disowned him and were disappointed in him, which couldn't have been further from the truth.

We stayed with our deal. When the four years were up, he ate a lot of hot dogs from the gas station and had to scrape by for three more years before his big break. There's nothing better than those kinds of lessons. He became even more serious about acting when he was hungry. Even his agent said she would have to let him go if he didn't book something soon. Sure enough, within two weeks, he booked his first role, playing Billy Graham in a movie called *Billy: The Early Years*. It was a small, independent movie, but I marveled at how he carried the movie in his first role.

He studied Reverend Graham's mannerisms and his voice diction. They styled his hair like him, put him in 1940s clothes, and he became Billy Graham. I always say that was my sign from God that this is what He has for Armie, and this was his tithe, his first fruit playing this amazing man of God.

We all went to the filming in Nashville. This "church lady" mom couldn't have been more blessed than if he had booked the largest blockbuster in the world. I mean, he was playing Billy Graham! Even his agent, Leanne, called me when Armie was going to audition for the role and said, "Your son was born to play this role. This movie is his. I know it."

After that, Armie booked his first big movie playing Batman in *Justice League*. They flew the crew to Australia to train and film. Six weeks into it, the movie was canceled due to being over budget. Armie came home completely devastated and defeated, but God had a better plan. He soon booked *The Social Network* and played both Winklevoss twins. He and the film were nominated for awards. His career skyrocketed. But remember, he wasn't an overnight sensation. All this new success didn't come without years of rejection and hurt, or worse.

Unfortunately, after many highs in his career, Armie was taken down years later. Bad influences and bad choices are a lethal combination. He began questioning God in high school. Michael and I didn't know at the time the depth of abuse he had endured in middle school.

In our minds, he was raised in a Christian, loving home. While nothing is perfect, we raised our boys in church and youth groups. We prayed as a family and read the Bible. We had lots of close family time. We didn't know where all this doubt and rebellion was coming from.

When Armie was bullied, his haven was his youth group. He lived for the Friday night youth group, where he had wonderful Christian friends, and the youth pastor took him under his wing.

This youth pastor was from South Africa and was so gifted in reaching that age group and making God relatable to them. He befriended us, went to dinner with us, came along on family vacations, and always seemed to have the best intentions for Armie and the youth group kids. But the wolf often comes in sheep's clothing.

We did not know he was grooming us—being our best friend so we would never suspect he would do anything inappropriate.

Suddenly, Armie said he didn't want to go to the youth group anymore. We had a wonderful young man, Dave, whom we called *Super Dave*, who worked for us and helped with the boys. He came to us and said the youth pastor had been inappropriate with Armie. We sat Armie down; he told us he had stopped anything from happening but didn't want anything to do with the youth pastor anymore.

Another lesson we have since learned is that when children are molested, they are ashamed and embarrassed and think it's their fault. Armie kept reiterating that nothing happened, but he did make him uncomfortable. We alerted the pastors, who called a meeting with the entire church, and they took responsibility. Other families came forward. There were several other boys he had molested.

We had him deported. Michael wanted to hire someone to kick his a** first. The level of anger you have when someone is hurting your child becomes illogical. This youth pastor will always be on the list of child predators in America, and he will never be able to come back to the States. We also alerted his home church and family of what happened. Hopefully, he will never be put in the position of being able to do that again to young boys.

We sent Armie to a Christian therapist. He went three times. Then he said to us, "Nothing happened. I don't need to go back to the therapist anymore. I've forgiven him." Thinking nothing physically happened, we complied with his wishes.

My biggest regret in the world is not being more proactive for Armie's well-being. Many years ago, we learned things *did* happen with the youth pastor.

Armie put it into perspective for me. He said, "Mom, even if nothing happened, you should have known that when a guy who is preaching Jesus even attempts something sexual to a child, it messes you up." How right he is. I feel like how I handled this situation is one of my biggest failures in life.

When speaking to parents, I often hear and have learned that children blame themselves. Sometimes, they say nothing happened because they are embarrassed, again blaming themselves.

I wish I could take it all back for a do-over. I would have been there more for my child. Children can blame God in that situation as well.

Why wouldn't they when a man in authority teaches them about the love of God and then does despicable things to them?

Why didn't I understand that? How in the world could I have not taken that a step further in my mind than even when abuse is attempted that psychologically messes with a child? How could I have thought, "Thank God nothing happened," and yet not think how that would mess a child up, possibly for life, if it was not dealt with? Certainly, in his childhood he didn't have the tools himself.

God created man, but He loves us so much He gave us free will. How are we going to live our lives? We either chose to live for God or chose evil. This youth pastor chose evil, and Armie went through years of dark stages.

Armie and I had no relationship for years. I would read his interviews and just cringe. I would leave messages on his voicemail, putting a little "Jewish guilt" on him, saying, "I birthed you, call your mom." He never did. He knew what I was calling about.

Finally, he was at the house one day, and I took his phone. Unbeknownst to him, I switched my contact's name from *Mama* to *Paramount Studios*. I waited a few days to call. Of course, he immediately picked up, thinking it was the studio–so busted.

I couldn't understand, even through the years following my divorce, how Armie and Viktor would have a relationship with their dad and not me. I understand now. First of all, Michael was the fun one. I was the skinny gray mess who was no fun and wasn't partying with them. Plus, I think Michael was poisoning them against me. Lastly, I think they also saw their father go off the rails, and they felt a need to be there for him. Michael was so distraught with regret after the divorce that he even spoke of hurting himself.

I never gave up on my sons even when they weren't speaking frequently to me. I told Armie and Viktor that I was praying for them and that I loved them. I would always call Armie out when he would speak to the press about things that were diametrically opposed to God's way.

Armie would get on a late-night talk show promoting his movies and say, "My mom is going to hate this story." So, I would pick up the phone and say, "You're right, son. I absolutely do hate that story, and I'm praying for you, and I'm begging you not to take the Lord's name in vain and tell stories (or live out those stories) that grieve God and will damage you."

My boys know what I believe. Other people may have the ability to keep quiet, but not me.

My dad would have held me accountable if I ever rebelled against God. I knew who he was from years of consistency and watching his faithfulness in living for Jesus. He was my rock in life.

I always knew I wanted and needed to be the rock in my children's lives. I just didn't know how solid I would have to be.

Let's pray together

Oh, God, how I love my boys. Thank you. When I felt like my entire family was taken away from me, You restored all. The joy You have given me when I m with my sons is incomparable to anything this world has to offer. Even when situations seem impossible, You are faithful. Amen

Chapter 19

Beyond the Headlines

I wish I could pretend the last four years didn't happen. Unfortunately, when you are at the grocery store, and the magazine trades are right in front of you with a cover glamor shot and the caption "I am married to a monster," there is no way to hide.

Armie made some bad personal choices that damaged his reputation and were hurtful to women. None of his choices were crimes. In fact, after an extensive look into what happened by the Los Angeles Police Department, all of the allegations were dismissed. Armie was cleared of all legal wrongdoing, but his moral wrongdoing was a different matter. The lingering effects of cancel culture endured, along with some broken hearts.

Much to his demise, Armie began exchanging messages with several women. The texting led to infidelities. The three women connected and banded together to go after Armie to destroy him in the press. One of the women charged him with sexual assault and rape. "Hell hath no fury like a scorned woman." You might have heard that saying. Armie lived it; therefore, we lived it.

It's not like it was the first time a leading Hollywood man behaved badly, but this time was different. The world had changed. Men behaving badly was being less tolerated by women. Cancel culture had just arrived and was permeating pop culture with great interest and fury. Armie found himself in the center of this new part of the pop culture zeitgeist. The consequences of Armie's choices were steep. He lost all of his work opportunities. He lost his ability to make a living. Armie was canceled.

I met two of the three young women who came against Armie. They were both beautiful and wanted way more than Armie was capable of giving them at the time. They were looking at Armie as Mr. Right. Armie was looking at them as Ms. Right Now. As a mother, my heart was broken for all involved. The covenant God has for two becoming one was not in this equation.

All of this unfolded at the beginning of covid when people were locked away in their homes. The feeding frenzy for new information was at an all-time high. It was the perfect storm. Every day, more and more articles were published. Yet, Armie stayed silent. At the time, he had decided not to talk to anyone for the sake of his family. The protective mother wanted to call him and say, "Let me loose. I saw what puppy dogs these women were with you. How could this be happening?" Instead, I also decided to stay quiet. It wasn't appropriate for me to defend Armie even though I fought the urge with every cell in my body. I prayed and mourned for my son and all involved. I prayed some more.

This might not be a popular view, but while I believe there is a large platform for women in the #metoo movement, I also know there are instances where women can say whatever they want with no recourse to themselves, even when accusations are unfounded. I take the stance of equality of the truth for men and women. We are starting the #usall movement, as everyone should have an equal voice.

I will never be the popular mom. I was never going to tell him, "Armie, I am throwing this out to the universe and thinking positive thoughts." There is a verse in the Bible that says, "Why would you worship My creation instead of worshiping the Creator." No, I was going to the throne room on my knees and crying out to the living God, Jesus. The only God who died on the cross for us and rose from the dead for eternity. All other gods are still in the grave.

Every one of us had major collateral damage at that time. A mother watching her son spiral, leaving a trail of broken hearts, and Armie's wife, Elizabeth, suffering with two young children, trying to survive the betrayal. I know the devastation of a broken marriage firsthand and the hardship that it puts on the children. When Michael and I divorced, Armie and Viktor were 22 and 24. Even at their adult ages, we all still plummeted emotionally.

No woman in the world walks down the aisle thinking, "I have a fifty percent chance of this working." Infidelity cuts deeper than anything in the world; I know, I've been there. The covenant of marriage that God ordained is meant to be sacred, "Do not let man separate what God has put together."

If you are going to stand up and be a Christian, you have to live it no matter what. Revenge or retaliation never ends well.

My sons moved all around, and we traveled all over when they were growing up. Was it as stable as the *Leave it to Beaver* home? No, but both my sons are the most well-traveled, independent sons, so it made sense that life was easier on Armie when his career took off and he was working all over the world. He was inspired by his work, and it's hard for any wife to live on sets. However, one thing I know from all my years is that it's hard to be separated for periods of time in any relationship.

There have been controversial things about the Hammer family dating back to the great-great-grandfather, who was a registered communist and went to prison for performing an abortion that went awry. Armie and Viktor's grandfather, Julian, well, let's just say, I never met or knew people like him even existed in this world, let alone would be in my family. His home was filled with pornography, pills, and drinking from early morning. Michael and another half-sister, Jan, who we love so much (she is a full sister in our minds), got the brunt of this growing up and lived with abuse.

There are generational curses from hurt being passed down. I know now that Michael's infidelities stemmed from a broken past that we never truly dealt with on a deep inner level. I had never been exposed to this, so I didn't understand that there are layers like an onion that need to be peeled away and dealt with. Those hurts can be passed down to future generations, or Jesus can break those curses and heal our innermost beings. It all depends on whether we want to "cast our cares upon Him," turn our lives over to Him, allow the bandaids to be ripped off, and let Jesus heal our hearts. I wish I knew then what I understand now.

This book has taken me nine years because I knew if I were to write this, I would have to be honest with "the good, the bad, and the ugly." Every family has all these, but I was thrown into the deep end, and thankfully, Jesus was my paddle. Armand has been gone since 1990, so no one would even give a flip about the Hammer family if Armie wasn't a successful actor.

To add more fuel to the fire, then came the Discovery+ documentary on the Hammer family instigated by Michael's sister, Armie and Viktor's Aunt Casey. Casey and her father sued Michael and me when Armand died. Armand left the bulk of his estate in the control of Michael, skipping Michael's father, Julian, who was Armand's only child–not a great recipe for a "big happy family". Armand knew Julian, with his addictions, was not equipped to handle responsibilities like this.

I was asked many times throughout the ordeal of the documentary to comment and tell our side, but Armie, Michael, Viktor, and I refused to comment, knowing the press would never give our side a fair shake. That was evident in the past few years. I knew the documentary was a work of fiction. Casey didn't know my family. She had not seen Armie and Viktor since they were little boys. She didn't know them at all. Yet, she was paid handsomely to tell a devastating depiction of my family, comparing Armie to Julian, who, I must be honest, truly was an abuser.

Once all the accusations came out and the so-called documentary, Armie remained completely silent. He didn't fight back. He didn't retaliate in the press. He just fought his hardest to be with his children when they were taken away.

Obviously, Armie got the brunt of the entire ordeal, but the press and documentary threw our entire family under the bus. There was collateral damage to Viktor and me on a smaller scale as well.

Then there are the occasional times when people have no idea my last name or who I am, and they do the cocktail conversations, jamming on how horrible the Hammer family is. I admit, I do get a kick out of saying, that's my family and seeing them shrivel on the vine. This is when choices in life become pinnacle—when the rubber hits the road. Are we going to let things like this defeat us? Or do we take it to Jesus, lay it at the altar, and believe what He says that no matter what we are going through "do not fear." The Bible says this 365 times, one for every day.

I had to cling to my faith even more so when another heartbreak hit. Michael was diagnosed with a Glioblastoma brain tumor, which has a life expectancy of a year or less.

Countless times, Michael would call me crying. Early on, after the divorce, he would call asking for my forgiveness. I gave it to him. I was always his stability. He would always say how proud he was of our sons and how much he loved them. He would tell me that because it's true—they are both smart and good, caring people. I can now admit that Michael is actually one of my heroes. Even with the abusive childhood he endured, he was still the most fun, amazing, and loving father and husband. I know he gave me and our family the best he could. We had a great life together, raising Armie and Viktor. I desperately wanted to have closure with Michael. After all, he was my husband of 25 years and the father to my children.

Just a few weeks before he died, I flew to Los Angeles to see him. When I walked into the hospital room, Michael was unconscious. However, when he heard my voice he let out a grunt. He knew I was there. I crawled up in his hospital bed and prayed over him, wrapping my arms around him while crying in gratitude. I thanked him for doing the very best he could. He loved Armie, Viktor, and me deeply and made life so much more fun than it would have ever been. I told him I loved him and I acknowledged what a wonderful father and husband he had been to us in so many aspects. I also reminded him that we would all have a reunion party together in heaven.

Michael died on November 20, 2022. God gave me closure, but little did I know I was going to be a disaster when Michael died.

I was shocked at how hard Michael's passing hit me, even after 13 years of divorce. All of the wonderful memories still keep flooding my mind. It's a mystery to me how we ended up here on this very day. We had a true love affair, and all the calls from him telling me how I was the love of his life and how he made the biggest mistake of his life still flooded back into my mind.

Both of my sons were very close with their father. Viktor spoke with him daily. He was always checking up on his dad. Viktor and his dad also ran the Armand Hammer Foundation together. He is my private child. Armie doesn't have that luxury in the career he has chosen. Viktor has chosen a life of not being in the spotlight, but don't think he got through his journey unscathed. Fortunately for him, his attacks were not publicized in the press, but as we all know, a problem is still a problem.

Viktor was wronged in another way during the last three years. I can't discuss the details in this book because the cases have not been adjudicated. Viktor and I walked through the trials of his life once his father fell ill. In my life, I've seen greed and money make people do crazy things; some people even try to take what is rightfully not theirs. I wish people would learn that money doesn't bring happiness. It only gives options.

Viktor desperately wanted to see his father's wishes honored at the time of his passing. Unfortunately, that would not come easily. He has been so committed to honoring his father's memory that I'm truly humbled.

There's no one better or more qualified than Viktor to make sure what the Hammer's built stays intact. I've had the honor of walking through the legality process with him. He has inspired me every step of the way.

I watched Viktor grow mentally and spiritually. He had a prayer partner, an incredible Godly gentleman, Mike, who walked through this trial with him as a spiritual father figure–talk about a mother's answers to prayers! I had the privilege of being Viktor's sounding board and tried my hardest not to preach to him. When it comes to my sons, I need a glue stick more than I need lipstick.

One day, I needed to go to Montecito to the family office to get some photos. I got a text from Viktor, "Mom, while you're there, will you pray over the building for me?" I read those words and started bawling. To me, nothing else matters.

The loss of Michael bonded my sons closer than anything else could have. They live in different worlds and have chosen different career paths. However, through this trial, they realized they each have unique strengths and are a great team.

Jesus didn't say to forgive only the small things in life, to forgive if deserved, or to forgive if you choose to. He just simply says forgive because He forgave us. I know my sons and I have asked for forgiveness for anyone we have hurt because we have chosen this path. I see the people God has destined us to be, come back to life.

Just the other day, I sent Viktor a text asking him a question, and he answered me, "Give me a Y, give me an E, give me an S," and I laughed out loud with joy because I saw his funny sense of humor back after all the sadness he's been through. God restores.

My sons now realized that together, they are a great team. The original Armand and his brother Victor were best friends and business partners. I watched the patriarch, Armand, at his brother Victor's funeral. He couldn't control himself. He walked up to the casket at the end of the service, threw his arms over the top, and wept out loud in front of all the dignified people in attendance. He didn't care. The best friend of his life, the one no one could ever replace, was no longer there with him.

Every family can go through a list of losses. I am not entitled to throw a pity party. Yet through all of the trials of this world, the simple truth the Bible stands on is, He loves us unconditionally. He is faithful. He is our hope. He is our provider. He is our healer. He is our restorer of all. If, and that is a big if, we are willing to say, "God, if You are real, reveal Yourself to me," He will. He is waiting for us to open that door to our hearts and say, "Come, Lord Jesus." As I've said to so many, "What have you got to lose?

In a crazy way, I thank the Lord for these battles because I can see what God is doing. He brought our family back together. His plans were accomplished through these trials. My sons are now calling me for prayer or just to catch up, which is a mother's greatest joy in life. I've always told Armie and Viktor, "You might as well just serve the Lord because you literally don't have a chance in hell with a praying mom."

There are many different kinds of healing. Our first and biggest healing is when we ask Jesus into our hearts as our Lord and Savior. That healing is our healing for eternity and our hope on this Earth. There are supernatural physical healings. When Jesus laid down His life on the cross, He said, "By My stripes, you are healed." We can confidently pray for supernatural healing because Jesus made the ultimate sacrifice.

There are healings from God, giving doctors the wisdom to know how to treat illnesses and diseases. Jesus also heals us emotionally, healing our hearts, which can come in many forms. He can help us forgive when it's too big for us, He can heal our hearts from devastating losses, He can fill the void of heartbreak, and He can give us peace in our lives that nothing on this Earth can give us.

God says, "I take the worst things in life and turn them for good." I either believe that or I don't—and I do. I wouldn't go back and change anything that has happened to our family. I am seeing my sons continually turn to God in tough times and thank Him in the good times. The very best part is that I am watching them reach out for forgiveness and forgive the people who have hurt them the most. That right there is the gist of this life. The biggest bonus in the last ten years is the gift of my two fabulous grandchildren, Harper and Ford. They are the joy of my life. I wake up every day thanking God for my family, that I love with all my heart.

The message of the Bible is not only that Jesus died for us. The message of the Bible is that Jesus rose from the dead to save us. As the song lyric is written, "Because He lives, I can face tomorrow." Indeed.

Let's pray together

Jesus, our family has walked through the fire. We all have. But hopefully, we come out better people because we decided to trust You in all we do. You never promised us a perfect life. Every heart has been hammered. What You have promised us is You will never leave us or fail us. You are a faithful and loving God. Thank you and oh, how I love You. Amen

Chapter 20

My Life as a Holograph

I wish I could say I fervently read the Bible my entire life, but I didn't. As a teenager, I was your typical tomboy who would rather be out playing ball with the neighborhood kids than reading. And studying— forget about it. Somehow, I survived because my parents led us into *their* personal relationship with God. My sisters and I saw them dive deep into the Word every day. They would teach us the scriptures, but more importantly, my parents led by example. I guess you could say I lived vicariously through them. When I went to college, I started digging in on my own.

I remember the first time the words of the Bible literally jumped out of the page for me. I was a senior in college, and I had never had a sip of alcohol. That's why I went dancing every weekend. The thought of drinking Diet Coke or my favorite, Tab, and standing around in bars just wasn't interesting to me.

One weekend, some of my sorority sisters said, "Dru, come with us and get drunk just once. No one can graduate college without getting drunk one time," they said. "You can see how much fun it is. We will protect you."

I decided to see what all the appeal was. Well, I barely remember anything. What I do remember was throwing up and waking up half-dressed in my laundry basket. I must have fallen in trying to get my clothes off. Now, if that isn't a sexy visual, I don't know what is!

So that next day, I picked up the Bible with a splitting headache from the bad, cheap wine. I just flipped it open to see where it landed. Boom! This verse jumped out at me: "Do not be drunk with wine because that will ruin your life. Instead, be filled with the Holy Spirit." (Ephesians 5:18, NLT) That moment was an epiphany for me that God still speaks directly to us today in daily situations, and He wants to guide our every step. Not only that, but why in the world would I not turn to the Creator of the universe, who knows the very best path for our lives?

From then on, I started reading and gleaning from the Word of God. I never felt the need to rebel against what the Bible said, no matter what society tried to say was "truth." God and His truth doesn't change. We are doing the same stupid stuff today that mankind has been doing since the beginning of time. How can the clay pot ever have the audacity to challenge the potter? I've seen the Word work. I have seen countless lives change because of learning God's ways.

Cancel culture would love to wipe Christianity off the face of the map. But all you have to do is read historically in the Bible what happened to cultures who tried removing God thousands of years ago. Their ending isn't pretty. Rebellion against God never ends well.

When I think of my grandchildren, two by blood and two others I claim as my own—and frankly, all children—I wonder how they'll access the Word of God in these changing times. Will they read their family Bible like years ago? Will they read the Bible online? Will the Bible become interactive in their lives? I certainly pray the Bible ignites the Truth in their lives. But it is our responsibility. God tells us, "Teach your children and your children's children." I take that personally.

Whatever format the Bible takes on in our post-industrialized, high-tech world, I know that the Truth within those pages is eternal and will never change. The message of love, hope, and forgiveness is more important than *how* the message is delivered.

When my sons email, text, or call me saying, "I love you, mama," I don't stop to think about how that message arrived. I'm just grateful the message came. The same is true for the Bible.

In April 2020, the world was shut down due to the response to covid. I happened to be living in Phoenix during those crazy days. I didn't feel stuck, but like so many people, I wanted to enjoy the outside air as much as possible. Arizona was a perfect place to do so.

People who know me well realize sitting around indoors waiting for covid to pass was not my style. I am a project-driven person. I like to do things that hopefully benefit others.

Phoenix also is the home base for Childhelp. I also thought maybe I could be useful to the children of Phoenix and beyond during this difficult time. So many people were being affected by covid and the shutdown in one way or another.

Typically, in Phoenix, I hung around with Sara and Yvonne, the co-founders of Childhelp, and my friend Scott, an extraordinarily talented Phoenix-based businessman.

During covid, Scott warmly brought me into his family. I quickly fell in love with all of them. We had dinner at least four nights a week. I rode my bike all over town, went to hit golf balls, and played with Scott's grandchildren, since I couldn't be with mine, because they were in the Cayman Islands. Having Scott's family was truly a blessing and a comfort during a very uncertain time.

What Scott didn't know is I never travel by myself. I always bring Jesus. Scott was a self-professed agnostic. He had no idea the "Drunado" that would be coming into his home telling him about Jesus. But he kept inviting me back, so I kept sharing. I took it as a good sign. Eventually, God came through for Scott—or maybe I wore him out! I can't take all the credit, though. It was actually my dad who ended up leading Scott to Christ. I tried for three years, but my dad ended up "closing the deal." I said to Scott, "What am I, chopped liver?" But as I know, some plant, some water, and some bring in the harvest. My dad and I made a good team, and God gets all the credit.

From that point on, Scott's entire paradigm shifted. He took to his new-found faith with the same fervor he did with his business. In fact, he started sending me Bible verses from his daily readings. He also shared Christ with business associates and friends. He sent me a picture of the new license tag he ordered. It was one of those "In God We Trust" license plates with the numbers 592022 on it. That was the day he asked Jesus to be the Lord of his life. If only all new converts would take the gospel and run with it like Scott has!

One day, Scott called to tell me about a story he saw on *60 Minutes* on an AI (Artificial Intelligence) project about Holocaust survivors. The AI company, a conversational- interactive platform, developed the project to preserve the memory of Holocaust survivors. Since the Holocaust happened in the 1940s, if the survivors were children, today they would be in their 80's or 90's. The company, along with Steven Spielberg and others, knew how important it is to remember the atrocities of human cruelty so, prayerfully, that history doesn't repeat itself.

I loved this idea of AI capturing the personal stories of Holocaust survivors, and I also thought it was an important step in remembering what the Jewish faith endured. Someone once said, "Only by knowing where we have been can we carve a path forward." I agree. I was absolutely blown away that AI would be able to create an everlasting memory of the survivors of such cruelty.

It was Scott's new-found commitment to the Bible that inspired him while watching that Holocaust story on *60 Minutes*. The AI company filmed Holocaust survivors being asked and answering 1,500 questions about what life was like during the Holocaust. What's fascinating is, the Holocaust survivors appear like a holograph, as if they are in front of you, sitting in a chair. It's truly like having a live, one-on-one talk. This AI technology blew my mind wide open.

Scott continued to explain why he thought of me during the TV piece. He said, "Only you could have convinced me that Jesus is the Messiah. I think you could use AI to spread the gospel and teach more people about what the Bible says." A light went off in my head. I thought Scott was on to something.

Being fairly certain I would see the goodness in this endeavor, Scott had already emailed the company before introducing it to me. And get this: they had already emailed him back and requested a conference call with us.

Scott may have been excited, but the more I thought about it, I thought he was crazy. Not because I had doubts about using AI for this purpose. That part was genius. Christians have been using some form of technology and ideas to spread the message of Jesus for a very long time—from before the printing press and beyond. Just think of when the internet first came around and how we used it to connect. The key, like with anything, is to be mindful that it is used for good.

What I thought was crazy was the thought of me answering thousands of questions on what the Bible says instead of a Bible scholar. I mean, I read the Bible, but I'm certainly no expert. Furthermore, the project sounded like the most overwhelming thing in the world. It's one thing to answer questions about your personal life, such as the Holocaust survivors had done, but it's another to have to answer what God says in His Word. I guess Scott can be as persistent as I am because he at least convinced me to get on a phone call with the head of marketing for the AI company.

When the day arrived, I asked Robert if he would mind if I prayed on the call before we got into business. I always do that. I'm up for anything if I know it's God's plan for me. Honestly, though, I hoped He would pass this one on to someone else! On the initial call, I said a simple prayer. I asked God to open the doors He wanted to open and close the doors He wanted closed.

Finally, I asked God to give me a sign if this was something He wanted me to do. I knew if I tried this on my own, it would be a futile endeavor. There was this long pause after I said the quick prayer with Robert and Scott, asking for sovereign guidance. I immediately thought, "Well, there you go, I've blown Robert away. He thinks I'm crazy." So, there was my sign. I was out of this!

Then Robert said, "I've never heard anyone speak to God with such simplicity and clarity. It's like you know Him.

Robert said, "I believe this is the project I was meant to do my entire life."

Ohhhh Lord, there was my sign. I was in this!

When I see young women who are pregnant for the first time, I always think to myself they have no idea what they are getting themselves into. Don't get me wrong, having children is worth it, but they have no idea. I should have been thinking the same thing about this AI project. It seemed like overnight, Jewels and I were researching and gathering well over 1,500 questions about the validity of the Bible from atheists, skeptics, agnostics, and various religions. The toughest questions were from children. For example, many of them asked, "Where are dinosaurs in the Bible? Were they on Noah's ark?" My team and I spent four months researching all these questions. I had countless pages that kept growing. Then came hours a day of studying. Plus, I was expected to remember all that I was studying!

The answers I provided are not my opinion. They are what the Bible says. If the Bible truly is the inspired Word of God, the "road is narrow," and I was venturing into hacking off a lot of people. I kept reminding myself, "Are we here on this Earth to run a popularity contest, or are we here to spread the Good News?" I forged on. All this preparation made me feel like I was wearing one of those heavy metal-laden blankets a dentist puts on you when you go in for X-rays.

When the date came for filming, I showed up all seven days, two hours early, for hair and makeup. I was so sleep-deprived from the weight of this project. Plus, the endless hours every night after filming, studying, and preparing for the 300 questions for the next day. Thanks to Eileen, my make-up artist, she basically had to put wallpaper paste on my face to disguise the bags under my eyes. For seven days, I was at the studio for at least ten hours, and for eight of those hours, I had to sit in a chair in the exact same position. I couldn't really move except for a few short breaks and lunch. After a few hours, the entire lower half of my body went numb, so it was a challenge just to uncross my legs. Then, question after question was thrown at me.

Now, you may be wondering, "Where does the AI come in?" That's after the filming. AI takes the questions and directs them to the proper answers. For example, you can ask the same question in ten different ways. "What day were you born?" can also be "When is your birthday?" or "How old are you?" AI simply spins the questions to the correct answers.

Anyone can access my new and exciting interactive website, gethope.ai, on a laptop or phone. Once you're on the site, simply push a button to ask a question. Suddenly, I will appear in front of you and answer your questions about the Bible.

After going through over 700 pages of edits, I still wasn't finished with my gethope.ai project. I knew that asking a few questions was great, but it wouldn't truly teach how God wants us to live this life. After all, the Bible is our manual guide from God on how He wants us to live our lives—which always begins with "Love the Lord your God with all your heart, mind, soul, and strength." (Mark 12:30, NLT) That's why I was inspired to go through the One Year Bible—365 days of teaching in less than 15 minutes a day (except for a few times when I just got too excited and long-winded and spoke more. But they are never over 17 minutes long!) These teachings can also be accessed through gethope.ai.

There are so many people, even Christians, who have never opened a Bible and have no idea what is in it. I had the advantage of growing up with parents who taught me and my sisters at a young age, so the Bible isn't intimidating to me. I liken it to my sons starting on ski slopes at ages 3 and 5. They were flying by Michael and me in the first year on skis. Being adults, we have this fear factor of plummeting down the slopes. The boys put the skis on, and away they went. There is that childlike faith, but starting as an adult can be intimidating. It's the same with anything. Please allow me to help you overcome that fear and walk with me through the Bible.

After deciding to take on this project, my team and I worked on a study guide that people can order on our website. Every day, there is an excerpt from the Old Testament, the New Testament, a Psalm, and a Proverb. We go through these together and hopefully bring in some interesting historical facts.

I filmed the tutorials from my iPhone, starting by putting it on my iron box—which has never been opened—and using a can of tuna fish to hold the phone up. It worked, but Kathie Lee told me, "You know, there are tripods that will hold your phone up in the right place." How ironic that the two most non techy people can still help each other. This new venture took off with many bad hair days and wrong pronunciations of those Biblical names, but it was off and running. Now that it's complete, my team and I believe in it wholeheartedly.

I figured if this Bible is truly the inspired Word of God and God is the Creator of the universe, then 15 minutes a day wouldn't be too much of an ask for people to learn. I am as guilty as anyone of skipping days because I am "just too busy." Yet, I seem to have time to eat, work out, and more. Hopefully, this study is a small teaching tool, amongst many wonderful others, for us to walk through the Bible and learn together.

I pray people will come on this journey with me. As I've said a few times already, what have we got to lose? If I'm wrong, then we are all "deader than doornails," as my mother used to say. But if I'm on the right path, we are promised eternal life with Jesus in Heaven and Heaven here on this Earth with a loving Father taking care of us, protecting us, loving us, and guiding our every step. We just have to open our hearts and say, "Come, Lord Jesus." That is a great gamble of odds in this life. I believe Jesus will reveal Himself to you as you dig into these teachings with me. He gives us H.O.P.E.

Let's pray together

Jesus, when things seem so impossible, that s when You do Your greatest work. We can never take the credit. You did more than help me through this project. You carried me through. It isn't easy. We have to do our part. Then You take it from there! I love you, Jesus, and thank you for trusting me in this project. Amen

TO CONTINUE ON THIS JOURNEY...

If you want to learn more and get involved, I'm launching four new projects.

Along with my new book, Hammered, here are the different projects God has given me:

www.druville.com is where you can buy additional Hammered books, and you can also find my colorful and whimsical druville products.

www.gethope.ai is an artificial intelligence (AI) interactive website where you can catch me answering all kinds of questions about the Bible. You can interact one-on-one with me. Once you're on the website, you will be prompted and given the opportunity to ask any question about the Bible, and I will answer you as a holograph! Some people are fearful of AI, so let's use it for good!

Also, on www.gethope.ai, you can join me for 15 minutes every day of the year. We'll walk through the Bible, and I'll share fun historical facts and explain some of God's mysteries. There are also journals on the www.druville.com website with my colorful designs so you can take notes, write your prayer requests, and journal what touched your heart that day. The journal also has highlighted notes from the day's teachings. Let's grow and learn the Bible together!

A large percentage of the proceeds from these passion projects will be donated to the Hammeredheart Foundation (www.hammeredheart.org) to help fund ministries and charities.

Thank you for all of your support, with gratitude and blessings!

Dru

Made in the USA
Columbia, SC
25 July 2024

7fc6cdce-acdb-4385-be9c-c4faa368f1d4R04